21st CENTURY GHOSTS

21st CENTURY GHOSTS

ENCOUNTERS WITH GHOSTS IN THE NEW MILLENNIUM

JASON KARL

First published in 2007 by New Holland Publishers (UK) Ltd
London • Cape Town • Sydney • Auckland
www.newhollandpublishers.com

Garfield House, 86-88 Edgware Road, London, W2 2EA, United Kingdom

80 McKenzie Street, Cape Town, 8001, South Africa

Unit 1, 66 Gibbes Street, Chatswood, NSW 2067, Australia

218 Lake Road, Northcote, Auckland, New Zealand

ISBN 978 1 84537 537 9

Although the publishers have made every effort to ensure that
information contained in this book was meticulously researched and
correct at the time of going to press, they accept no responsibility for
any inaccuracies, loss, injury or inconvenience sustained by any person
using this book as reference.

Some of the photographs in this book have been enhanced, and do not
necessarily portray actual apparitions.

Editorial Director: Jo Hemmings
Senior Editor: Charlotte Judet
Researcher: Sian Rayner
Designer: Luke Herriott at Studio Ink
Jacket Design: Alan Marshall and Phil Kay
Production: Hazel Kirkman

Reproduction by Pica Digital Pte Ltd
Printed and bound in Singapore by Star Standard

10 9 8 7 6 5 4 3 2 1

Jacket pictures: Mary King's Close, Edinburgh (front); Pluckley (back).
Right: Mary King's Close. Pages 6–7 (left to right): Main's Hall, Charleville
Forest Castle, Dalston Hall Hotel, The Cleveland Ironstone Mining
Museum, Pluckley, Sandford Orcas Manor.

This book is dedicated to my parents, Elizabeth and Barrie, for never
disapproving of my spooky adventures!

CONTENTS

FOREWORD 8

INTRODUCTION 10

Case 1
THE CASTLE OF WHISPERS 14
Cornwall, England

Case 2
AT HER MAJESTY'S PLEASURE 18
Cornwall, England

Case 3
THE HAUNTED HOLIDAY COTTAGE 22
Devon, England

Case 4
CAUGHT ON FILM 24
Devon, England

Case 5
YO-HO, YO-HO,
A HAUNTING LIFE FOR ME! 28
Devon, England

Case 6
ALL MANOR OF SECRETS 32
Dorset, England

Case 7
GHOST ISLAND 38
Isle of Wight, England

Case 8
PATIENTS FROM THE PAST 44
Isle of Wight, England

Case 9
THE ANTIQUARIAN APPARITION 48
Surrey, England

Case 10
MOST HAUNTED? 50
Kent, England

Case 11
THE SPECTRE IN THE CHAPEL 70
Gloucestershire, England

Case 12
IN HARRY PRICE'S FOOTSTEPS 74
Suffolk, England

Case 13
GHOST IN THE MACHINE 78
Warwickshire, England

Case 14
THE PHANTOM HITCHHIKER 80
Shropshire, England

Case 15
HOUSE OF HELL 82
Lancashire, England

Case 16
LILY'S STORY 86
Lancashire, England

Case 17
THE PSYCHIC MUSEUM 92
Yorkshire, England

Case 18
HORROR HOTEL 96
Yorkshire, England

Case 19
THE CHILDREN OF THE MINE 100
County Durham, England

Case 20
THE SPECTRE INSPECTORS 104
Northumberland, England

Case 21
TOUCHED BY THE DEAD 108
Cumbria, England

Case 22
WALLED UP ALIVE 114
Pembrokeshire, Wales

Case 23
GHOSTS OF THE FORGOTTEN LANE 118
Edinburgh, Scotland

Case 24
A FACE IN THE WINDOW 122
Falkirk, Scotland

Case 25
TERROR TOWER 124
Fife, Scotland

Case 26
HIDDEN HAUNTS 126
County Offaly, Ireland

Case 27
THE HAUNTED GITE 130
Vendée, France

Case 28
THE MONK OF CARCASSONNE 132
Languedoc-Roussillon, France

Case 29
TORMENTED SOULS 136
Westphalia, Germany

Case 30
THE HEARSE WHISPERER'S TALE 138
Sydney, Australia

Case 31
THE CASE OF THE HAUNTED DOLL 140
Florida, USA

Case 32
THE HAUNTED MANSION 144
Michigan, USA

Case 33
SHADOWS IN THE WINGS 148
Wisconsin, USA

BE AN ARMCHAIR GHOSTHUNTER 152

DIRECTORY OF GHOSTHUNTERS 152

BIBLIOGRAPHY 156

ACKNOWLEDGEMENTS 156

INDEX 158

FOREWORD

By DEREK ACORAH – the UK's most famous spirit medium

I was flattered to be asked by Jason Karl to write the foreword for his latest book, *21st Century Ghosts*. Jason and I worked together on the first series of LIVING TV's programme, *Most Haunted*, and during that time I came to respect and admire him in spite of the fact that we were investigating allegedly haunted locations from opposite sides of the fence. Jason is meticulous in his scientific approach to investigations and his input into the world of parapsychology is important – more important perhaps than those who, being attached to academic institutions, are somewhat narrow in their views and will never be able to look at the subject of parapsychology with the open-mindedness of those who, like Jason, view the subject from an entirely unbiased perspective.

The perception of ghosts drums up pictures of castles and manors, ancient crossroads echoing with the groan of long-gone gibbets, creaking old houses and darkly haunted hollows where spectral highwaymen lurk for eternity in wait of their unsuspecting, but never to arrive, victims. Although our land boasts more haunted locations of age than any other country in the world, let us not forget that ghostly apparitions are not the preserve of the past. Nor are they confined to this country alone. From the four corners of the Earth come stories and reports of paranormal events and ghostly sightings.

In his poem 'Clouds', Rupert Brooke said: 'They say that the dead die not, but remain near to the rich heirs of their grief and mirth.' In other words, life goes on. When we leave our physical bodies, we continue on in the world beyond in spirit form and sometimes, when we feel drawn back to our earthly links, we revisit the places and the people who were important to us during our lifetime here on earth. You are just as likely to experience seeing the spirit presence of a person who you have known in your lifetime as you are likely to see the ghostly apparition of a long-gone inhabitant of an ancient building. This is the reality of my belief and I prefer to think that parapsychology is attempting to prove rather than disprove that reality.

I have been working as a spirit medium for 28 years now. For the last 12 years I have been involved in investigative programming where I have been taken to numerous allegedly haunted locations. During this time I have been amazed at the rate that worldwide public interest in the paranormal has grown. Whereas not so very long ago a person's perception of ghosts and hauntings was confined to threats of the 'bogey man' if we misbehaved as children, or the offerings of Hammer House of Horror films on television or at the local cinema, now I am astonished at the number of people who are truly interested in investigating the paranormal. With that interest has grown the number of people who are now prepared to speak of their ghostly experiences, where once they would be afraid to talk about such a subject for fear of being thought hysterical or slightly strange. They would have been embarrassed to tell even their closest friends that they had seen a ghost. But 'ghosts' or 'spirits', however you prefer to describe them, are as real as you and I.

From the mid-1990s and through to the 21st century, there have been more encounters reported by people who have experienced ghostly sightings than at any other time in history. It is important that these encounters are documented in order that we can all share in the experiences and perhaps visit the locations ourselves. Jason's book, *21st Century Ghosts*, fulfils this need admirably. Because of the greater interest in the paranormal, people are now far more enthusiastic and, thanks to the work of Jason and others who work in his field, far more knowledgeable.

Derek Acorah
June 2006

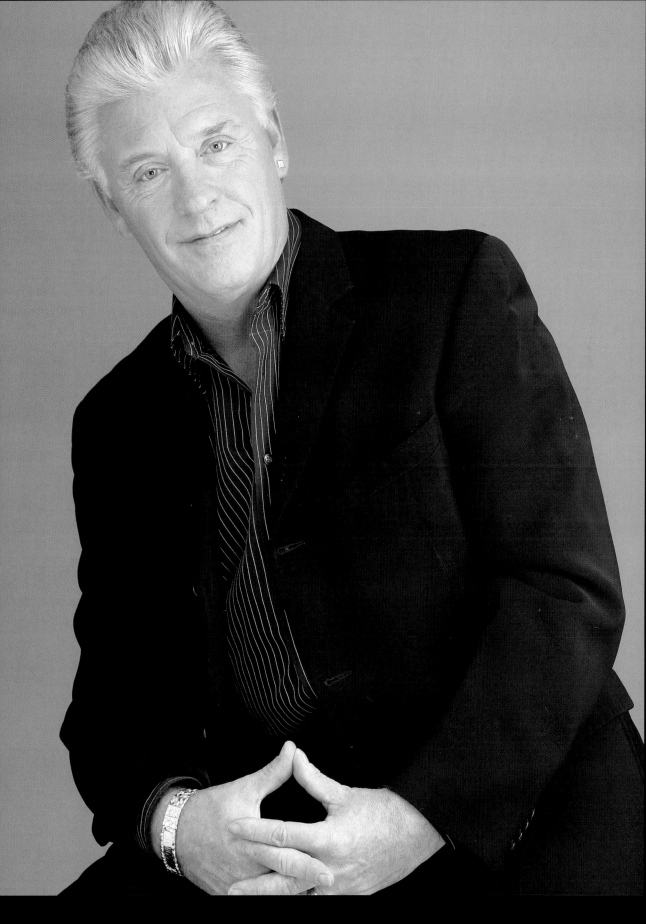

INTRODUCTION

Ghosts do not exist. Ghosts cannot exist. At least that is what the scientific community has been telling us for decades. Without proof positive that there is a way for us to survive bodily death, acceptance of ghosts by scientists, and therefore the wider community, cannot happen. Or can it?

Since the age of 13 I have been fascinated by the realm of ghosts and hauntings. A world that surrounds us and is for the most part unseen, and yet is sometimes glimpsed for a few precious, and occasionally terrifying, moments. The ability to 'see' beings from an existence beyond our own is termed 'psychic awareness', and there are those that will tell you it is only a special, privileged few who can tap into the invisible world – the spirit mediums, the psychic visionaries and the witches. I have found, however, that this is not the case.

Throughout my travels into the unknown world, seeking spirits far and wide across all continents, countries and cultures, I have discovered that it is more likely to be those that are not purposefully seeking phantoms that will actually encounter them. An encounter with a ghost might catch you unaware in your place of work, your home or on the street. Perhaps the person you have just watched walk down the road was not really there – at least not in this life. Ghosts are all around us and it is believed that one in ten people are likely to see a ghost in their lifetime; I wonder how many more people will not actually realize that they have seen one?

Since the turn of the new millennium, and the dawning of the forthcoming Age of Aquarius (in which it is thought humanity will transform from the spiritually oppressed Piscean age of religious orthodoxy, into a more spiritual harmony of universal peace and brotherhood) interest in the paranormal world, and particularly in life beyond death, has been on the increase. It is accepted by astrologers and those following the New Age that in the Age of Aquarius there will be a blending of religion and science, so that the two opposing views become one and a new spiritual truth will come to the fore. In a universe filled with technology and science, we are drawing back and the inner voice is calling us to 'slow down'. It is in these quiet moments of reflection that we examine our own beliefs and life experiences, discovering that despite being told we should not believe in something, actually we do.

The media world has latched onto this new 'paranormal consciousness' and serves up a feast of TV, DVD, internet and film offerings which all focus on the strange and unusual. Celebrities, too, are keen not to miss out with magazine features and books that tell of ghostly encounters and paranormal experiences flying off the shelves. TV presenter Richard Madeley told the Sunday Mirror that he watched a phantom coach and horses near his home in Hampstead, London, before it disappeared. Joanna Lumley recounted a tale of meeting a ghost in a house she once owned. Ghosts have also elevated themselves from the traditional crumbling castle or cobweb-filled manor house onto the flights of British Airways, at least according to Psychic News, who published a story concerning a ghost which was making regular appearances on a jumbo jet. But it is not only those in the limelight whose

tales become public knowledge. During a train journey from London's Waterloo station to Havant one sunny afternoon in June 2006, a graceful lady in a Victorian dress was observed by a fellow passenger. While at the Thistle Shopping Mall in Stirling, Scotland, the ghost of a little girl has been recently witnessed, along with disembodied footsteps and voices in empty storerooms.

The past, it is said, will come back to haunt you, which certainly seems to be the case at the Lenin Museum, Moscow. The director of the museum, Maja Obraszowa, told the world's press in 2006 that the building was being visited by the ghost of the former dictator. The bed in one of the rooms often shows signs of being slept in, despite the building being locked and alarmed each night, and the smell of apple cake wafts around, even though no bakery exists for many miles. As you might have guessed, apple cake was Lenin's favourite dessert.

In the USA, the wraith of former president Ronald Reagan is thought to be haunting his ranch high in the hills above Santa Barbara. At the Rancho del Cielo, a hacienda-style estate, a figure riding a galloping horse has been seen near the perimeter of the property, along with poltergeist behaviour in Reagan's former bedroom.

For this project I have selected a contrasting variety of cases from around the world which show, beyond all doubt, that even in our science-based society, things that we cannot explain do happen. In each case file the testimony of the witness is accompanied by photographs of the location in question, in some cases these pictures themselves contain imagery which is hard to explain. The tools of science, usually working to disprove theories of the supernatural are now working in its favour, after all the camera does not lie … or does it?

My intention with this book is not to prove to the sceptics that ghosts exist, or to pander to the 'ghost obsessed' who accept everything they see as paranormal. Instead, the evidence is provided for the reader to make up his or her own mind. Contained within these pages are testimonies from private individuals, ghost hunters, spiritualists and investigators who have each offered their story in good faith, and I have accepted each story as a truthful recollection of a genuine experience.

At the end of the book you will find details of how you can become an armchair ghost hunter yourself and also, for the first time ever, a directory of ghost-hunting societies around the world. The true ghost fan will find this an excellent resource and a way to network with like-minded individuals.

As you explore these pages, and walk with the living in this haunted world, take a moment to consider where you might return to if you had the chance after death. I have often pondered this and gone so far as to record my hoped-for destination – after all, the psychic explorers of the years to come would have a good place to start if they had a record of where people 'intended' to haunt once their time in this life is over. It is a sobering thought, but we could be the ghosts of the future.

Jason Karl, July 2006

If you have had a ghost encounter anywhere in the world, I would like to hear your story. Who knows, it may end up in a future publication. You can contact me through my website at www.jasondexterkarl.com

Above: The lonely tower of Pengersick Castle, perhaps one of the UK's most haunted castles, hides a plethora of phantasmal residents in the rooms behind its unassuming exterior.

THE CASTLE OF WHISPERS

LOCATION: Pengersick Castle, Cornwall, England

DATE: July 2003

TESTIMONY: Stuart Andrews, Paranormal Research Organisation

There are those who are convinced that things which go bump in the night are definite signs of ghosts, or contacts from beyond the grave, while there are others who think such stories to be exactly that – fiction and no more. One thing that I feel able to state conclusively is that I have witnessed both believers and sceptics experience things that they cannot explain while visiting Pengersick Castle in Cornwall.

Set in beautiful grounds and barely half a mile from the wild west Cornish coast, there is an air of magic to the castle, described by many as 'where the veil between this world and the next seems permanently thin'. During every visit I have made to Pengersick over the last seven years, something inexplicable has occurred. Indeed, what has struck me the most about this famously haunted building is that, although unexplained phenomenon often happen, the same occurrences are not guaranteed every visit. There is always something new to be encountered.

The following is an account of one of the most paranormally active investigations I have ever attended at the castle. It was also my first investigation since joining the Paranormal Research Organisation and I had a team mostly comprised of relative newcomers to the ghost-hunting scene. Many have noticed that activity seems to be at its highest when 'fresh blood' is inside the castle, and I certainly agree that often visitors get their most intense experience on their first visit. Regular ghost nights are run at the castle, for those of a brave disposition.

I have felt a strange force or presence in certain areas of the grounds each time I have visited. Previous groups have also noticed this and members of the groups I have led have also commented on feeling unwell, dizzy or giddy in the same areas, without any prompting or prior knowledge. The most severe of these occurred during this particular investigation in July 2003.

While touring the grounds, a dowser and myself both independently tracked a presence following us, without the other knowing. Then, in the area of the plague burial pits, a sharp constant pain developed in the right of my chest, which passed after half an hour or so. At first I presumed I might have drunk too much coffee setting myself up for the night. However, it transpired that other people have also experienced this pain. I also saw what appeared to be the head and shoulders of a figure moving between the trees, which is another common sighting I was not aware of as most of my

previous investigations had centred on the castle tower. I immediately ran down to the area where I had seen this figure, and using a high-powered torch scanned the area, flooding it thoroughly with bright light to make sure there was not an intruder on the grounds and not surprisingly no one was there.

A previous investigation resulted in an incredible phenomenon being caught on video film. The shadows of what appear to be rats running along the ground. This was witnessed by a whole team at the same time as it was being filmed. Sadly, this has been a one-off occurrence and we were not privileged to see such a sight during this investigation.

Pengersick Castle has a colourful history which is littered with tragedy and whispers of sorcery and death. This has led to the creation of many legends about the Pengersick family, the castle and its ghosts. The building as it stands today dates back to the fifteenth century and would be more correctly described as a fortified Tudor manor. The tower forms the main part of this new building, and was actually built with reclaimed stone from the original castle which was situated at the far end of the present grounds. This explains why the phenomena reported in both the castle and grounds are often so similar, begging the question of whether or not they are caused by the same ghosts. The most active rooms during this investigation were the solar and the bedroom – so called because it is the only room in the tower featuring a magnificent four-poster bed. Many of those in the groups that I have led here have immediately said that they feel something in certain areas. In particular, that they are drawn to areas of the bedroom without knowing why. This pattern repeated itself again on this occasion despite nearly all those present being totally unaware of the previous accounts. One could argue that certain areas of any room will feel less or more inviting than others, however, when visiting the castle at night you know when a feeling is picked up on or have an experience, because often it is not at all what you were expecting.

A wandering wisp
Other strange experiences include pitch black anomalous forms seen moving around the bedroom, sometimes in the shape of a figure, or more commonly in the shape of an arm or leg. A particularly impressive light anomaly was captured by Anthony Simms, and is the best I have ever seen. All I can say is that there were no lights moving around within the room and there was definitely no one smoking at the time. This 'wisp', for want of a better description, moves up from the floor, changing brightness and speed as it moves up the centre of the video screen, then it changes size and apparent density. It finally returns to more or less its original appearance. At one point it looks like a haze of smoke and I was really unnerved watching the tape back to see it start to follow the contours of my body before moving away and disappearing. I am at a loss to explain this and have not captured anything similar before or since, which makes this investigation really stand out as an eventful one.

There was a further event which was also a first to my knowledge. It was experienced by the two sceptics in the group, who were both forced to reconsider their beliefs as a result. While waiting on the lawn for the rest of the team to return from the last vigil of the night, a figure was seen by both investigators, walking along the path from the gate which runs past the side of the castle to the main door. At first they thought it was me. Confused, they immediately contacted me on the two-way radio and asked me to confirm that the rest of the team were still in the bedroom, which we were. Concerned that this might be an intruder and knowing that the owners were all in bed, I sprinted down the tower stairs and flung the door open but no one was to be seen. Described as being approximately five and a half feet tall and male with light-coloured, wispy flowing hair, this did not match the description of any of the team or the owners. I am totally confident that this sighting was not due to an intruder either because the area was thoroughly flooded by torchlight and there simply was not time for someone to have disappeared naturally.

Even if you are a non-believer it is impossible to dismiss the idea that something strange is happening at Pengersick Castle. Many professional dowsers have identified the same areas I have referred to as having spirits present. Indeed, there are major ley lines that pass close to the castle, via nearby St Michael's Mount, which run through the southwest up to other locations of paranormal significance, such as Glastonbury Tor, in Somerset. Could it be that these ancient energy sources may be felt or picked up by visitors? As an alternative argument to ghosts and spirits, could ley lines be the cause of the strange feelings and apparitions experienced by so many?

For further details about the Paranormal Research Organisation take a look at their website at www.paranormalresearch.org.uk

Details of Pengersick Castle, including how you can take part in a ghost hunt at the castle can be found at www.ghosthunting.org.uk

Left: All that remains of Pengersick Castle is the former Pele Tower, and of course, its many ghosts...

Above: Partially derelict, and devoid of inmates, the one time prison of Bodmin Gaol has held onto the spirits of those it incarcerated over a 200 year period.

AT HER MAJESTY'S PLEASURE

LOCATION: Bodmin Gaol, Cornwall, England

DATE: April 2005

TESTIMONY: Dave Wood & Nicky Sewell, Paranormal Site Investigators

During the seventeenth century an imposing gaol complex was built in the picturesque and unassuming Cornish town of Bodmin. Over nearly 200 years, thousands of prisoners passed through the gaol where they suffered terrible conditions often for trivial crimes and misdemeanours; for example, the starving were incarcerated for stealing livestock. Over 50 inmates were executed at the gaol and many premature deaths were caused by the harsh regime and living standards. The gaol was the site of England's last public hanging, which attracted thousands of people, so requiring the extra provision of train carriages from all mainline stations. After the decommissioning of the gaol in 1927 the site fell from prominence until it was chosen to house the Crown Jewels, Doomsday Book and other national treasures during the Second World War. Since that time, the townsfolk have variously made use of the complex as a public house, a restaurant and a nightclub.

The gaol in its various guises has attracted tales of ghostly activity for as long as anyone can remember. Encounters have included the ghost of a female prisoner who was hanged for the murder of her son. An angry man has been seen in the Naval Gaol and further apparitions have been sighted throughout the complex.

On 2 April 2005 researchers from Paranormal Site Investigators descended upon the gaol with the intention of assessing whether the buildings really deserved their spooky reputation. The well-trained team was equipped with an armoury of monitoring equipment, a sound scientific methodology and a sceptical approach. Some of the PSI's most unshakeable and field-hardened investigators stayed overnight within the infamous compound. The team were literally locked in until dawn. PSI was joined for the night by a BBC television news reporter, whose aim was to objectively and responsibly document the night's investigation.

Prior to the commencement of the investigation baseline measurements and recordings were taken throughout the premises, in order to allow the investigators to identify any fluctuations or trends throughout the night's proceedings. This process involved investigators utilizing a wide range of environmental monitoring equipment to record readings such as temperature, humidity,

electromagnetic fields and negative ion density. These readings were recorded and studied throughout the night by the group because of their suggested effect on people's perception and their suggested alteration as a result of unexplainable phenomena.

After this process was completed, the group undertook a séance in the ruined Naval Gaol. This area is now an imposing four-floor high shell. The group was situated at the base of a honeycomb of moss-ridden door-less cells, stretching for several floorless storeys into the heavily blanketed night sky, with moonlight offering the only illumination to the group of intrepid investigators below.

Group founder, Nicky Sewell, led the team in their first attempt at contact with whatever tortured souls may have still remained within this area. Asking for any spirit presences nearby to come forward and make themselves known, it was not long before Nicky and her team were about to experience the first of many such encounters during the night.

A sneering smoker appears

Initially, the minutes dragged by as the group stood in the sharp night air. The hardened investigators expected little from this first session, knowing as they did from past cases that the likelihood of any substantial experience is always very low. Two members of the group were startled to see what appeared to be several faint, moving figures at the darkest end of the Naval Gaol. Only a little time had lapsed between this sighting and the chance to report it before two different investigators spotted something more substantial and less fleeting. A clear figure was seen leaning against a darkened cell door, just feet away from the assembled group. With what appeared to be a lit cigarette dangling from his lips, this figure sneered arrogantly towards the team as they asked him to step forward. As the figure appeared to vanish and the investigators returned to a posture of tense expectation, one of the more toughened members suddenly fled from the Naval Gaol, overcome by emotion. She was accompanied to safety and recounted that even with years of investigations under her belt she had never experienced anything of this magnitude. She told of an overpowering sense of oppression, which evoked within her the necessity to leave the area to protect her physical and psychological wellbeing. The remainder of the team were not far behind her, as one by one they felt a sense of malevolence consume the Naval Gaol, unrivalled by anything previously experienced. Séance leader, Nicky, was the last investigator to remain within the building, seemingly unaffected by the overwhelming sensations that had caused her team members to leave. It was not long, however, before Nicky had her own encounter with the sinister forces residing within Bodmin Gaol.

Making their way through the labyrinth of cell floors and corridors, the team split into two groups. Team leader Dave tackled the lower cell floor, with colleague Nicky taking her team to the middle floor.

Accompanied by the BBC television reporter, Nicky's team began taking equipment readings on the middle floor. Once the readings had been recorded, the group plunged themselves into darkness as the session began. Sensing movement towards the end of the room, Nicky prepared to take a photograph. As on all investigations, she said 'flash' to warn fellow investigators to close their eyes. Instead of a camera flash following her utterance, the group were alarmed to hear Nicky call out as though in shock or fright, and the room was rapidly illuminated by the concerned investigators. Crouching down to the floor, Nicky pointed towards a stone about five centimetres long and three centimetres wide resting at her feet. Nicky went on to claim that the stone had seemingly been thrown at the back of her head as she gave the 'flash' warning. The group immediately measured the temperature of the offending article and recorded it to be 10°C. They went on to measure the ceiling temperature, which was recorded at 7°C, and the floor at 5°C. The team deduced that the increased heat detected on the stone suggested there could have been an energy source behind the stone, which would account for its temporary kinetic ability. As Nicky knelt to note down these recordings, she was shocked once more to hear a stone skim across the floor towards her, which, on testing, also recorded temperature levels considerably higher than the surrounding area. Radioing through to Dave's team on the lower floor, Nicky requested their presence to help her team come to the bottom of the mysterious stone throwing activities. Upon the other group's arrival, the two teams began a thorough inspection of the middle floor and found that the stones that were moved or thrown did not appear to come from the ceiling of the cells, therefore the likelihood of the stone simply falling was unlikely. They found that both the ceiling and walls appeared to be structurally sound and were left bewildered as to what may have caused these incidences or from where the stones originated.

Left: The gaol complex incorporates several buildings, some still in use by the living, as well as the dead...

The stone throwing continued throughout the course of the investigation, irrespective of the team's location and always centred on Nicky. On each occasion, the stone and surrounding area was thoroughly investigated. Although most remaining sessions were conducted in partial light, the team were unable to see the stones in transit, only ever seeing or hearing it land, therefore preventing the team from ever discovering the stone's origin. The team packed up and were let out of the gaol at dawn, making the long trip home to begin their analysis of the night's events.

Bodmin Gaol remains the group's least explicable case. Although the apparition sightings could be the result of primed expectation in the context of a spooky environment, the stones hurled at the team are less easy to explain away. The BBC TV camera, which was trained on Nicky, captured one of the occasions the stones were thrown but the source of the stone was not visible. The significantly higher spot temperatures of the stone compared to the temperatures of all the surrounding surfaces suggests that the stones did not simply fall. The enclosed rooms of the complex, with video cameras trained on entranceways, meant that outside interference was virtually impossible.

The only possible explanation offered by sceptics has been deception. A member of the team holding the stone in their hand and then throwing it. However, the trained and trusted team would have nothing to gain from this, and the team could have only lost out by a deception taking place in front of television cameras. Paranormal Site Investigators always try to rationalize and explain in all cases, but the case of Bodmin Gaol seems to have stumped our scientific method.

For more information on PSI – Paranormal Site Investigators and their activities – take a look at their website at www.paranormalinvestigators.org.uk

THE HAUNTED HOLIDAY COTTAGE

LOCATION: Margells, Branscombe, Devon, England

DATE: September 2005

TESTIMONY: Suzanne Williams, Witness

My husband and I booked into the Landmark Trust's cottage, Margells, in Branscombe, for a four-night break between 25 and 29 September 2005, little knowing that it was reputedly haunted. We had hardly unpacked our bags before we had our first strange encounter. We were both sitting at the dining table in the kitchen when out of nowhere a tremendous 'whoosh' sound, followed by an almighty crash, was heard. We both looked at each other blankly but put it down to the house next door (which we later found out is inhabited by a single elderly lady who is unlikely to have made such a racket) and thought little more about it, although I must stress at this point that my husband did not like the atmosphere of the house as soon as he entered.

Later, I was reading the guestbook and learned of previous holiday-makers' supernatural experiences. I purposely, therefore, left the sitting room, kitchen and landing lights switched on all night, plus I wedged open the kitchen and sitting room doors to prevent the ghost opening them as had been reported in the guestbook.

We slept in the front bedroom on the first night, which has a medieval painted wall and a vaulted ceiling. My husband went to sleep almost immediately but I was uncomfortable and found it difficult to settle down. A short while after I had been trying to sleep I noticed a peculiar blue light which appeared in the eaves. I thought perhaps this could be explained by the landing light being left on, but it seemed such a piercing blue and white colour that I remain unconvinced that it had a natural cause. My husband was disturbed in the early hours of the following morning by loud bangs which he felt were 'not of this world'.

On the following morning we were both suffering with flu and so were confined to the house, which had a heavy and depressive atmosphere throughout the morning. The kind of feeling where something is not quite as it should be. As the afternoon progressed we became increasingly anxious and as the twilight engulfed the house an incessant tapping as that of a 'cane' on the floor was heard in the sitting room, which was later accompanied by swishing sounds. During the early hours of the morning our bedroom door latch had been lifted and dropped by something invisible, and later the bathroom door latch did the same.

Frightened away

The next morning we decided to cut our holiday short and leave Margells and its ghostly residents behind. After spending a few hours on the beach we returned to the cottage to rest for a short while before beginning our journey home. At 4.09pm I was disturbed from a snooze by a thunderous crash as though someone was tipping or throwing furniture around in the sitting room – that was enough and with that we were off for good.

We did not find the spirit friendly as stated by other guests, in fact we felt it was antagonized by our presence and became more active the longer we stayed. I would never have intentionally booked a holiday in a haunted house – we just wanted a quiet holiday in Devon. People I have mentioned this to think that it must have been exciting to have been in the presence of a ghost. I found it more like an endurance test, and certainly something I would not wish to experience again.

Margells is owned by the Landmark Trust and is available for holiday lets through their website at www.landmarktrust.org.uk

The name of the witness in this testimony has been changed to protect her identity.

Above: Irrefutably the
most haunted inn in the
West country, The
Highwayman at Sourton
hides a multitude of
ghostly secrets.

Right: This strange image
was caught by The Ghost
Research Foundation in
2002, minutes after the
investigators had witnessed
unexplainable footsteps in
the haunted corridor.

CAUGHT ON FILM

LOCATION: The Highwayman Inn, Sourton, Devon, England

DATE: May 2004

TESTIMONY: Martin Finch, Witness

Since The Ghost Research Foundation carried out the first official investigation of this haunted inn, which stands on the edge of Dartmoor in Devon, in October 2001, the building has become known as 'the most haunted inn in the West Country'. It is a title it well deserves because it is home to a variety of colourful spectres that flit among the living unseen in this building of many wonders.

It is not really possible to put into words the experience of visiting this haunted building. Handcrafted over many years by Buster Jones – father of current proprietor Sally Thomson, who runs the establishment along with her husband Bruce – it is, as one journalist described it, a fairy-tale fantasy touched with pirate ship, church, museum and junk shop.

It is a place of curiosities and the jigsaw puzzle of its architecture, drawn from many sources, combines with Buster's vision to create a remarkable tourist attraction which amazes and amuses visitors from all over the world. They come knocking on the door every day, asking to see the 'most unusual inn in England'.

The original building dates back to 1282 and over the centuries a variety of ghostly tales have sprung up. Some of which are based probably on rumour and some on fact. What is indisputable is the experience of my visit in May 2004 when my wife Alison and I enjoyed a memorable stay.

Alison experienced some mild, yet unexplainable, occurrences. The first was the sensation of someone, or something, stroking her neck as we slept in one of the bedrooms known as the Victorian Room. I decided to take some photographs of the room before we went downstairs to enjoy one of Bruce's excellent cooked breakfasts. Little did I know at the time that I was not alone in the room.

When we returned to the bedroom after breakfast to pack up our things, Alison noticed that the cushions, which she had arranged neatly on the settee earlier on, had been flattened down, as if someone had been sitting on them. When we quizzed Sally about this she assured us that no one had entered the room. The next strange thing was when we returned home and downloaded the digital photographs I had taken. The one of the Victorian Room has a clear image of what appears to be a foggy moving figure. It seems remarkable that I managed to capture this ghost, even though I saw nothing at the time.

The Victorian Room at The Highwayman Inn is not usually regarded as one of the most haunted chambers in the building, yet this strange image was caught by holiday-makers Martin and Alison Finch in May 2004.

One of the most well-known hauntings is that of a ship's captain named Gravill who haunts the Galleon Room, now used as the dining room. The room is constructed from the remains of a real shipwreck in which 13 sailors died. The other ghosts include a cavalier named Samuel. He has been seen many times throughout the building and is thought to have died here following the Battle of Sourton (1643), in which he fought. One notable appearance of this spirit occurred on Halloween 2001 when he was seen taking part in a fancy dress party, although wearing a very different type of costume from the party theme.

Mysterious footsteps

Other well-attested phenomena include footsteps in deserted rooms. One such incident occurred while the Ghost Research Foundation was investigating the building in July 2002. On this occasion the team were enjoying breakfast in the Galleon Room when suddenly the quiet was interrupted by the loud sound of boots walking on the floor above them, yet no one was on that floor. The team rushed upstairs and began taking photographs of the area, hoping to catch something which was unseen but might show up on the photographs later. Sure enough something strange did appear. Known as a 'vortex', the swirl of light which can clearly be seen on the otherwise deserted corridor was not

Below: This 'vortex' photograph was taken by the Ghost Research Foundation. The picture was taken with a camera that does not have a strap attached.

Right: Taken by Martin Finch in 2004, this incredible image appears to show a figure in one of the inn's bedrooms. Martin was alone in the room at the time, or at least he thought he was...

visible to the naked eye and is thought to be the second stage of a spirit manifestation taking place. Sceptics might suggest that this is the camera strap obscuring the lens, but no strap was attached to the camera at the time.

If you are brave enough to visit The Highwayman Inn, details of opening times and overnight accommodation tariffs can be found on their website at www.thehighwaymaninn.net

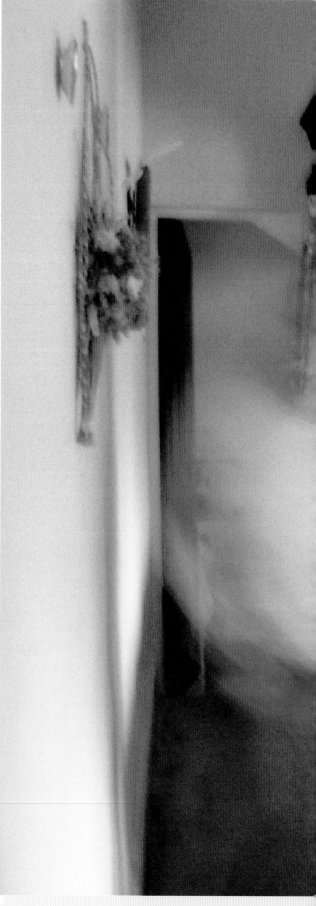

Above: The Smuggler's
Haunt Hotel is well known
for ghostly happenings, and
has a deserved reputation
as a haunted hotel.

YO-HO, YO-HO, A HAUNTING LIFE FOR ME!

LOCATION: The Smuggler's Haunt Hotel, Brixham, Devon, England

DATE: February 2006

TESTIMONY: Stuart Andrews, Haunting Experiences

Situated in the beautiful coastal town of Brixham, Devon, The Smugglers Haunt Hotel is just a stone's throw away from the harbour. It claims to have several resident ghosts, with both visitors and owners, past and present, regularly witnessing strange happenings. The inn has a notorious history of smuggling which may account for its many documented sightings and paranormal events. Even some of the most sceptical people have walked away puzzled about their experiences during their stay at this atmospheric place. Haunting Experiences run all-night ghost hunting events for charity, so this type of investigation is different to others because the team is mostly comprised of members of the general public with little experience in paranormal investigations. What made this night so unique and interesting was that the findings of the guests tallied so well with what has been reported before, and this was not divulged to them until after the investigation. Furthermore, one room in particular held a few firsts even for us experienced investigators.

Lots of peculiar things allegedly happen in bedroom 17, including light bulbs frequently blowing, fire doors opening, and the owner being physically shaken. On the night in question this was the quietest of the bedrooms for all the groups, with very little paranormal activity occurring. However, two separate groups picked up on an elderly lady who was identified through dowsing as being in her sixties. One group further revealed that she had moved things in this room and was standing near the kettle. Unknown to us at the time the kettle had previously been reported as a centre of poltergeist activity. It has been turned off and unplugged on many occasions, yet on returning to the locked room it has been found plugged back in and boiling. Hotel guests have also reported seeing an old lady sitting in a rocking chair, despite the fact that there is no such chair in the room. While these events were not very dramatic those who reported the old lady by the kettle had no way of knowing that this had been previously seen.

Bedroom one is believed to be where a child was placed in the chimney and subsequently died. Knocking noises are often heard here and light anomalies have sometimes been caught on camera and camcorder. One group reported hearing a knocking noise at the door as if someone was there, only to find nobody outside. The building was secured and two-way radio contact confirmed that there was no one walking around. A clicking sound was also heard by one group by the fireplace and many commented on how uneasy they felt here. One group identified a young girl who claimed to have lived

in the building and fell to her death from a window. Many locals do talk about the ghost of Aggie, a young girl who jumped to her death from an upstairs window 70 years ago. The room has now gone and the window would be where the utility room now exists. Was this the spirit heard in bedroom one?

Resurrection Bob

In bedroom seven a medium has previously picked up on a smuggler who was seen 'stuffing' things into the attic above. This is interesting because there is no attic there now and it is a flat roof. Some suggest this may link with the most famous of all Devon smugglers, Bob Elliott or Resurrection Bob, who is said to have owned one of the two cottages that now makes up The Smuggler's Haunt Hotel building. He escaped arrest by faking death and being placed in a large coffin carried out from the carpenter's shop, which is now the reception. He was then retrieved by his accomplices and was seen by coastguards who at first presumed him to be a ghost. Many found this room to be cold and uneasy and the level of activity seemed to increase here. Feelings of a presence being near were reported, accompanied by electromagnetic field fluctuations and temperature drops – one of 6°C. This occurred while one guest investigator felt something touching him while lying on the bed. We also recorded what appears to be a young girl saying 'One, Two, Three…', which is very interesting with respect to the findings from bedroom one and the girl who jumped to her death. Just as we were leaving and had switched the lights back on, the negative ion detector went off the scale and continued to give high readings for nearly a minute. In the years that I have been investigating using this piece of equipment, this is the first time I have recorded a reading of this magnitude. Many believe a change in the ion count within a room indicates a possible spirit presence. Perhaps the spirit was asking us not to leave or maybe it was showing its approval that we were going.

The most active area of the hotel on the night was undoubtedly bedroom six. Most of my group saw flashes of light with the naked eye. This was the only room in which such a phenomenon was reported. Noises were also heard from behind the closed bathroom door. The spirit of a man in his thirties was identified through dowsing methods. He had been a free trader – a smuggler or pirate – and had been killed by a rival and buried at Berry Head. It was further discovered that he apparently moves around as a ghost and makes noises. There was a large amount of light anomalies or 'orbs' caught on camcorder here, so we decided to try disturbing dust particles by moving towels and so forth in the hope of explaining some of these, but without success. With no insects in the room, could this have been what some people claim to be spirit energy?

Many reported feeling sick or light headed in bedroom six, including two of our guides, Ian Addicoat and Kevin Hynes, who reported being touched by something unseen. This is perhaps best described in Ian's own words: 'The feelings began on my shoulder and then my face. At one stage they stopped and without any prompting from me the lady to my right suddenly exclaimed that she was feeling the same.

Right: Ghostly goings-on are not confined to one room at The Smuggler's Haunt; you may encounter the resident spirits in the bar...

It was as if the spirit had moved from me to her. After a while her experience ceased and it returned to me once again. The sensations moved right across my body and down my left arm. Suddenly they ceased for a second time and then Kevin Hynes began feeling a tingling on top of his head. When they left him a lady further along felt sick, another felt tingling and then two others felt tightness in their chest and sickness.' This was all most unusual because I have never known Ian to report such phenomena despite many years of investigating together. I was later to have my own similar experience in this room.

The level of activity in here had been high throughout the night, but it was still an unexpected shock to witness one of the sceptical guest investigators suddenly faint in the room, following an increased level of activity being reported by those present. Once he had recovered we made our way back to bedroom six, where, during a final séance experiment, three people, including myself, reported a strange obnoxious smell, which was likened to human vomit. While sitting in the same area that Ian had earlier reported being touched, I was surprised to feel as if someone pressed two fingers down on top of my right thigh and later I felt this again on the side of my leg. This was the highlight of the night with three of the four seasoned investigators present reporting physical contact in the same area of the same room. Something we have never experienced at any haunted location before.

I might have expected a few guests to experience more activity later on in the night due to tiredness. However, this proved to be the most active part of the night, in direct contrast to most findings which usually show a clear tail off of reported activity. I am still left with the question of why the upstairs and bedrooms six and seven in particular were the most paranormally active, while the downstairs was quiet throughout the night. Could it be that the ghosts who haunt the Smuggler's do not confine themselves to the one room and choose where they will make themselves known as and when they feel like it?

For information on Haunting Experiences see their website: www.hauntingexperiences.co.uk

For further information about The Smuggler's Haunt Hotel visit
www.smugglershaunt-hotel-devon.co.uk

Above: Sandford Orcas Manor House, once regarded as one of the UK's most haunted places, was visited by a spiritualist medium in 2005.

ALL MANOR OF SECRETS...

LOCATION: Sandford Orcas Manor, Dorset, England

DATE: September 2005

TESTIMONY: Veronica Charles, Spiritualist Medium

The Tudor mansion at Sandford Orcas near Sherborne stands proudly among the haunted houses of our land. It has altered little over its 350-year history and is said to be the haunt of numerous ghostly presences. Its reputation as one of England's most haunted houses has been somewhat damaged by claims in recent years that a previous owner embellished the stories in order to attract visitors to the house. This may or may not be the case but there is never smoke without fire and the haunting history of Sandford Orcas can be traced back as far as 1908.

Virtually every room in this mansion was at some time reputed to be haunted by something or somebody, and even the grounds have not escaped the attention of those on the other side. One of the most enduring ghosts at the manor is that of a psychic echo described as sounding like the musical notes of a spinet or a harpsichord, which linger on the breeze around the old gatehouse area. The gargoyles which sit atop the roofs of the building are said to bear a ghostly grin in the moonlight, while malevolent phantoms tread the corridors of the house. The ghost of an eighteenth-century farmer has been seen on regular occasions, wandering past the kitchen window. He is alleged to have hanged himself from a trapdoor in the manor, and his restless spirit still walks there, dressed in a white smock. In one account a Mrs Smith claimed to have seen him on 29 December 1966, at approximately 3.40pm. She described the apparition as semi-transparent and moving in a strange bobbing and floating motion unnaturally high above the ground. Her husband also caught a fleeting glimpse of the ghost, and a dog reacted by barking madly at the door in the direction of the sighting. Colonel Claridge – the then tenant – informed Mrs Smith and her husband that this was a common occurrence and that the figure passed that window on an almost daily basis, each time causing the dog to react in the same way. Another ghost outside is that of an old Gypsy woman wearing a mackintosh. She was once seen coming in through a garden gate and disappearing around a corner. When followed she could not be found but her coat was later discovered hanging in a garden shed.

Inside the manor the ghosts take on a more malevolent nature, with the upper rooms the most affected. Two anniversary ghosts haunt the master bedroom. The first is a sinister Moor who was a servant who committed murder in the house and who now visits for seven consecutive nights during July, manifesting daily at 2am. The second is a priest who killed his master in the bedroom and is reputed to

haunt on a yearly basis. Both ghosts are said to stand beside the bed and stare at those sleeping in this haunted room.

The benign phantoms of six cowled monks were sighted in an upstairs chamber on 5 October 1971 – the Feast Day of St Francis. They were seen at 7.30am and arrived in two sets of three. The tenant's dog took an instant dislike and is said to have attacked one of them. There is also a Woman in Black who is the spectre of a former housekeeper who busies herself preparing rooms for guests. Her soul is glimpsed flitting from one room to the next, going about her business as if she is still in the land of the living.

The former staff wing is home to two unpleasant ghosts. There is a Georgian footman who allegedly preyed on young girls and serving maids during his life, and continues to do so after his death. His manifestation appears as a sinister seven-foot figure and has been enticed to appear by ghost hunters bringing virgins into the house. He is said to be particularly attracted to those under the age of 20 and comes out of the gatehouse before focusing his haunting activity on the staff wing. The second phantom is that of a young man who was locked up in a room here on nights of the full moon. For the rest of the time he was free to roam the village but his character changed upon a full moon so much so that he killed a boy in Dartmouth. The piteous cries and screams of this lunatic still echo around the room in which he was imprisoned, the far bedroom at the end of the staff wing. One account states: 'and when the moon is up we hear the most fearful screams from that part of the house. This is either the girls being raped by the vicious Georgian Footman, or the madman screaming to be set free.' Sandford Orcas Manor is not a place to be on the night of a full moon.

Lady in red

The spirit of an old lady was once seen by two female visitors who were sitting in an upstairs bedroom, in which there is a fifteenth-century bed that once belonged to Catherine of Aragon. She was recognized later from a portrait in another part of the house. One room is kept chained up and locked, because whenever it has been opened all manner of poltergeist activity has resulted with the entire contents of the room thrown onto the floor. The stone staircase just outside this room is visited by the Red Lady, a woman in a hand-painted silken gown. In years past a red silk dress was found in an old chest in the attics and speculation has it that the garment belonged to the Red Lady. Ghost hunters have recorded anomalous sounds here, believed to be the voices of three children and an old lady with a spinning wheel.

There is equally little peace in the downstairs quarters. The great hall is occupied by the spirit of Edward Noyle. The Noyle family lived here until 1748 and Edward was responsible for many architectural alterations to the manor. His ghost is one of the few benevolent entities at Sandford Orcas and is reported to stand and stare out of the windows opposite the Tudor fireplace. A ghostly dog called Toby also haunts this room, appearing each 15 September, who died in 1900 and is now buried in the orchard. Another ghost downstairs is that of a seventeeth-century man in a black cloak and hat, who has been sighted in the vicinity of the old kitchen, now the dining room.

Sandford Orcas is a building crammed full of psychic wonders, with rattling chains, a room where it is impossible to take photographs, an unidentified Old White Lady, a room that 'screams', a spectral white horse and the tormented staff wing where 'the stench or decomposing flesh impregnates the walls every night'. It is surprising that the Paraphysical Laboratory, following the study in the late 1960s identified only 5 ghosts, while 14 is the total quoted in other texts and by my reckoning there are 25 lingering spirits in this haunted mansion.

When I visited the manor in early September 2005, accompanied by a group of ghost hunters, I was asked for my psychic impressions of the house. Having worked as a spiritual medium all my life I was expecting to be deluged by the spirit activity which I had been told took place at the manor. It was a hot and humid afternoon with an overcast sky, which cast a gloomy shadow over the building as we entered. We were greeted by the owner, Sir Mervyn Meddlycott. Sir Mervyn took the first opportunity to tell us that the manor was not haunted, and that all the stories had been fabricated by his former tenant. It seemed to me that he protested a little too much.

We began our tour of the ancient house, accompanied by a peculiar sound which emanated from the pocket of one of the ghost hunter's coats. It was a 'ghost radar', which is a gizmo that records changes in the atmosphere which might indicate a paranormal presence. The sound was clearly heard by other people on the tour, but no one commented. I am sure that Sir Mervyn would not have approved.

The manor is brooding and very atmospheric. As we made our way up the spiral staircase and into the upper chambers of the house I was gripped by a psychic sense that we were not alone, unseen eyes were upon us. The sensation was strongest as I entered the bedroom that lies on the right-hand side of the entrance porch as you look at the front of the house. The bedroom had a huge four-poster bed and was thick with the atmosphere of ghosts. I sensed two discarnate entities here, of a lady and a gentleman. The female was a dominating character, very controlling, while her companion was a more passive, happy-go-lucky sort of person. The feeling exuding from him was that he was made unhappy during his lifetime at Sandford Orcas by the presence of the overpowering lady. I sensed that he was a kind and gentle soul at heart, keen on black Labrador dogs, which he used to keep, and generous to servants. The woman was jealous, greedy and of Mediterranean, Italian or Spanish extraction. An image of a dark-skinned woman with long flowing black hair and a sense of a gypsy filled my vision. She was not from the aristocracy but from a peasant background.

As I moved towards the fireplace the sensation grew stronger, and the image grew in my mind. She had married a gentleman and had been 'made good' by him. Her greedy hopes had been fulfilled when he had asked her to marry him, but this was not a happy marriage. After she had ensnared him, she had insisted on separate bedrooms, leaving him with only his Havana cigars as company. The result was a 'wandering eye and soon a young maid had caught the husband's attention. It was in the servants' wing that one dark night an illegitimate child had been conceived and eventually a disabled child was born which was hushed up. The maid had been discharged soon afterwards, but not before she had

had the sense to furnish herself with some valuables from the manor which she could sell to feed her newborn.

The spirits of the lady and the man were strong in my vision, but there was a third phantom in the bedroom, that of a black cat – the dark lady's pet. It was then that I glanced at the window to the left of the fireplace and noticed a strange star-shaped symbol in the stained glass – the symbol of witchcraft. A shiver ran down my spine, and as I looked around the room, which was now almost empty of people as they were moving on to the next chamber on the tour, I wondered if this dark lady had been a witch. The black cat could have been her magical familiar and the gypsy vision in my mind's eye was perhaps a clue to a bewitching secret.

I have not been fortunate enough to spend a night inside haunted Sandford Orcas. When I contacted Sir Mervyn Medlycott to ask for permission he informed me in writing that in his opinion there are no ghosts at the manor and that there never have been. As the owner I respect his view but it is hard to ignore so many reports of strange happenings and the pervading sense of terror and torment in the manor. I know I glimpsed a shadow of it in September 2005.

Above: St Catherine's Lighthouse has been investigated by prolific researcher Gay Balwin since 1990, with astonishing results.

GHOST ISLAND

LOCATION: St Catherine's Lighthouse, Isle of Wight, England
DATE: 1990 - Present
TESTIMONY: Gay Baldwin, Ghost Hunter

By day the Isle of Wight is a place of sunshine, spectacular countryside, beaches and various leisure activities. But it has a darker side. For it is also notorious as the most haunted island in the world – Ghost Island. This small island, just off England's south coast, is home to hundreds of ghosts and supernatural happenings. The island has a long and rich history and so it is not surprising that ghostly goings-on and haunting echoes of turbulent past times continue to reverberate into the twenty-first century

From phantom monks, grey ladies and poltergeists, to the shades of smugglers, soldiers, royalty and Romans, there are ghostly murderers and their victims, ghost ships still sail the seas and ghost trains still run on vanished rails. Hundreds of unquiet and restless spirits haunt hotels, hospitals, manor houses, pubs, shops and offices, while the spirits of countless smugglers and shipwrecked seamen still walk lonely beaches.

At the most southerly point of the Isle of Wight stands St Catherine's Lighthouse. This white octagonal tower has 94 steps to the lantern, whose beam can be seen by ships up to 26 nautical miles away. At almost one million candlepower it is the third most powerful light in the Trinity House Service. Now unmanned and controlled from Harwich, the lighthouse has been automated since July 1997, although it is still open to the public at certain times, with tours licensed by Trinity House.

There has been a lighthouse at Niton since 1323, when local landowner Walter de Godyton was ordered by the Church, as a penance for his role in smuggling activities, to build a lighthouse on St Catherine's Down, and pay a priest to say Mass for the souls of shipwrecked mariners who came to grief on this dangerous coast. A brazier in his 11 m (35 ft) high octagonal tower was kept burning, and the remains of St Catherine's Oratory, known locally as the Pepper Pot, can still be seen today.

As a lighthouse, however, it was not a great success, for frequent thick fogs obscured the feeble light and ships still hit the treacherous rocks below. The wreck of the Clarendon in Chale Bay in 1836 with the loss of 24 lives so shocked public opinion that construction of a new lighthouse, near sea level at St Catherine's Point, was started in 1838.

The original tower, which stood 36m, was too high for fog still obscured the light, so in 1875 it was reduced to just 26m. In 1932, the St Catherine's foghorn, with a range of ten miles, was moved from

the cliff edge to a low replica tower in front of the lighthouse and these two towers are known locally as the Cow and Calf. The foghorn was discontinued in 1987.

The lighthouse has been continually in service since 1875, although during the last war its light was extinguished to prevent enemy bombers using it for navigation and only lit when convoys were due to pass. Tragedy struck on 1 June 1943, when the very last local air raid of the war nearly put out the light forever. The damage this raid caused to the original 1840 lead crystal reflector glass can be seen to this day, as can the poignant last entry in the watch keeper's log.

Eight Focke Wulf 190s launched a surprise attack on Niton, coming in at sea level one misty morning. Their target was probably the radar and wireless stations located there. But the large Undercliff Hotel, where service personnel were billeted, was completely demolished instead, with the loss of two lives. At the nearby lighthouse the death toll was higher. A bomb that missed its target fell instead on the emergency power house and boiler room, where the keepers were stacking bird perches they had just taken down from the tower. Tragically, all three men, R. T. Grenfell, C. Tomkins and W. E. Jones were killed and lie buried together, in the local churchyard at Niton. A polished brass memorial to them is displayed in the main lighthouse tower.

The mysterious man at the window

BT telephone engineer Les Fletcher was not aware of those events 50 years earlier when he arrived to install a new telephone system in the lighthouse one winter's day in the early 1990s. 'I was working there alone. The Keeper, Frank Creasey, had left me to finish and lock up when I left. It was late in the afternoon and growing dark when I tested the system, collected my tools, and left the empty tower, locking the door behind me. I thought the lighthouse looked quite dramatic in the gathering dusk, so when I reached my van I found my camera and shot off a couple of photographs a few seconds apart.' It was not until Les had the film developed several months later that he noticed something odd at the top of the lighthouse. This appears in the second of the two prints. There, clearly outlined against the window of the tower, stands the dark figure of a burly man.

'I couldn't believe my eyes,' said Les. 'There was no one else in that tower with me and when I locked the door I know the lighthouse was empty. I have puzzled over those photographs for years but can't explain them. Reluctantly I have come to the conclusion that it's a ghostly keeper who stands there … and he's still on watch.'

Researcher and author Gay Baldwin adds: 'The photographs were taken with a 35mm camera (not digital) and I am currently in possession of the negatives. These have been carefully examined by photographic experts, who have confirmed that they have not been tampered with in any way.'

When Frank Creasey examined those photographs in July 2004, he, too, was puzzled by the strange figure in the tower, especially as he remembered Les working in the lighthouse and confirmed that he had been there alone. A keeper with Trinity House for over 30 years, Frank has served at several of Britain's best-known lighthouses, including those at Eddystone and the Needles. He moved to St Catherine's Lighthouse as a keeper in 1985, and after the lighthouse was automated continued there as an attendant, living in the house at the base of the tower with his wife, Shirley. Although he has been alone in the tower many times, a rather sceptical Frank has never seen that phantom figure. He does, however, reluctantly admit to sharing his home with a noisy family of at least three ghosts.

Ghosts in a hurry

Lighthouse Dwelling as it is known, was originally the battery house and tower entrance. After the wartime tragedy it was converted into the Principal Keeper's house, although it was still the tower entrance and a thoroughfare for visitors. It is here, in their hallway, that Frank and Shirley hear, but have never seen, the ghosts of a man, woman and young girl playing out a small domestic drama.

'We hear the mother talking to her daughter in a low voice. We cannot make out the words, but from the urgent tone of her voice she is clearly trying to hurry the little girl up. We then hear her trying to pull the child to the door, but the girl is protesting because she wants to wait for her father. Then comes the sound of a man's footsteps following behind. All three go out of the front door and it slams shut.

'That front door is locked and bolted, but we still hear it slam when the ghosts leave. It's so odd. We only hear them leave and it's always the same, rather like a video loop, which replays at intervals. Sometimes we can go for a year or more without hearing them.

Left: The beacon of St Catherine's Lighthouse, where a ghost was caught on film.

Right: The 'pepper pot', as it is locally known, was the forerunner of the current lighthouse, and dates back to 1323.

There's no recognisable pattern; it doesn't happen on any particular date or time of day. Although we can't make out the words, we have heard them so often over the years that we can almost understand what's being said.

'It doesn't worry us at all. Although we don't see the ghosts we know when they are about because our cat watches them, staring fixedly as they move around the living room and hall. The only time we have ever seen anything was when we bought a swing-top rubbish bin for the sitting room. They didn't like that. We would be in there of an evening and that lid would start swinging. They would play with it all the time. Finally, while we watched, the bin was kicked over. We got rid of it after that.'

As well as appearing in Les Fletcher's photograph, one of the lighthouse ghosts was captured on CCTV early one morning. Frank explained: 'In the summer of 1999 a young chap called round to apologise in case he had disturbed us during the night. The man, who was staying in a nearby caravan site with his brother and girlfriend, had been to a party and after a few drinks they had decided to have a look at the lighthouse. At around 1am, while clambering over the wall, his brother had fallen and the others had climbed over to help him.' They were sorry if they had made a noise and woken Frank, and apologized for trespassing too.

But Frank already knew what the nocturnal visitors had been up to, for he had observed their drunken antics on the lighthouse security cameras. 'I could see all four of you quite clearly lit up in the spotlights. I even watched you lighting a cigarette,' he laughed. Then added, 'Who was the fourth chap with you?' 'There were only three of us,' the visitor assured Frank. So to settle the matter Frank showed him the security video. Four people, three men and one woman, were clearly visible on the film. However, while the three party-goers could be seen scrambling over the wall, the fourth figure, that of a man in dark clothes, appeared around the corner from the front door of the lighthouse to join them, before walking off towards the wall again.

'I don't know who on earth that was!' said the young man in astonishment. 'There were only the three of us there,' he insisted. 'We never saw him at all, yet on the video he's standing right next to us. That's weird. Perhaps you've got a ghost here,' he joked. There's many a true word spoken in jest...

Gay Baldwin has been investigating ghosts on the Isle of Wight since 1977. She has written six books on the island. To read more, visit her website at www.ghostisland.com

Below: Les Fletcher's Photograph: In this image, taken in the early 1990s, a solitary figure can be seen standing behind the glass at the top of the tower; yet no-one was in the lighthouse at the time...

PATIENTS FROM THE PAST

LOCATION: Ventnor Botanical Gardens, Ventnor, Isle of Wight, England

DATE: September 2005

TESTIMONY: Paul Gerfen, Myths, Ghosts & Legends

We have our fair share of ghosts on the Isle of Wight. Whether you believe or not in the world of spirits, this little island has plenty of paranormal hot spots. There is no more haunted a spot on the island than the southwest area, and one location sticks out more than any other – Ventnor Botanical Gardens. It was here that the Myths, Ghosts & Legends team decided to investigate.

Our team consists of six members: me, Janis, Lisa, Ben, Jason and Karen. We have two believers, Janis and Jason, while the rest of us could be called sceptics. We have a wide range of ghost-hunting equipment, but prefer not to involve a medium. We like to experience any paranormal activity ourselves without intervention from those that profess to have psychic abilities.

Ventnor Botanical Gardens is without doubt one of the most heavily researched haunted sites on the island, due to the amount of alleged paranormal activity that occurs on an almost daily basis. Although today it is a beautiful botanical garden snuggled under the cliff of Ventnor, most of the bumps in the night can be put down to the hospital that once stood on this site.

In 1861 the Royal National Hospital for the Diseases of the Chest had just opened its doors for the first time. It was decided that Ventnor was the perfect location for such a large and important hospital. The fresh sea air would heal the chest and lungs, while the cliffs high above helped to shelter the building from high winds. Every ward had its own balcony and the patients would be wheeled out in the morning and brought back in during the early evening.

The building served as one of the main hospitals on the south coast of the island for over 80 years. Unfortunately, as is only expected in a hospital, many patients who stayed there did not live and were wheeled away through one of the hospital's underground chambers to the hospital morgue. In 1969, following many years of neglect, the building was finally demolished. Plans were already fully developed to replace it with a beautiful park, full of colourful flowers and exotic plants.

Since it was first created, visitors to the park have often reported feeling watched, touched and followed by ghosts. Some have even seen full apparitions of patients from the past enjoying a walk around the former hospital grounds. Despite the building being flattened and the underground tunnels being sealed, some people have reported feeling strange at a certain spot in the present-day car park.

Strangely, this spot lies right over the tunnel to the morgue, which now lies many feet below them – entombed within concrete.

It was a reasonably warm cloudy night in September 2005 when our team decided to try and experience some paranormal activity in the gardens for ourselves. We armed ourselves with an electromagnetic field meter, digital thermometer, MP3 recorder and an infrared video camera. Lisa took some base readings of the area, to determine the 'normal' levels of temperature, electromagnetism and so on, but of course being outside we were unable to record accurate readings easily. The ambient temperature was 16°C and we could find no evidence of any sources of natural electromagnetic energy.

One of the well-known paranormal hot spots is the former nurses' tunnel. Although the entrance is bricked over, you can still partly see the underground tunnel leading up from the gardens through the cliff into the staff house high above. It was here that Jason first remarked that something had caught

Below: Beautiful by day, the area takes on a sombre atmosphere when the moon shines brightly over the haunted gardens.

Below: The pathways that weave through Ventnor Botanical Gardens are used by both the seen, and the unseen.

his attention out of the corner of his eye. Although the five of us did not see it, Jason said he saw a small ball of bright light slowly drift around the entrance of the tunnel before dispersing into nothing. Unfortunately, the cameras were not focused on the exact spot, and the EMF meter did not show any sign of unusual electrical activity.

When we reached the middle of the garden, the rose arbour, both my wife, Janis, and Jason reacted to hearing a heavy wheezing sound. They said it came from the space right between them. Luckily, we had the MP3 recorder with us. This device not only records everything but also amplifies the sounds for the listener. Ben confirmed that he, too, had heard something, although he was unsure exactly what it might have been. Later on that night I was able to download the sound file and listen to it for myself. Although you cannot really make out a definite sound, you can see there is a noticeable difference in the sound wave. The pitch of the white static noise really does change quite considerably. You can hear this clip for yourself on our website (see below for the address).

We headed back towards the car, not expecting anything more to happen, when the EMF meter suddenly let off a shriek. For a brief few seconds it registered a high anomalous reading. The signal quickly dissipated and we tried to find a cause for the incident, but we could not. We made sweep after sweep of the area, but nothing was found. It was then that we realized where we were standing – over the former morgue tunnel.

Lisa decided to take some temperature readings in the area, but bizarrely the thermometer refused to give an accurate reading. It was fluctuating wildly between 2°C and 7°C and took several minutes to stabilize. Upon reflection this could have been caused by a natural phenomenon such as wind affecting the ambient temperature, but that does not explain the electromagnetic spike above the morgue tunnel.

Although the garden had let us down with proof positive on the night, it still is no doubt a very active place. Reports still come in daily of ghostly sightings and strange events. You cannot help but feel some of it is due to the very nature of the gardens. Being a botanical garden, you do come across some very strange smells, for example, the smell of chloroform is commonly reported. Unfortunately, as we found out, this can be put down to a certain type of plant that gives off the smell mainly at night. There is no doubt that the garden has a lot of secrets, but I guess for now we will have to be happy with the electromagnetic anomaly.

You can read about more of Paul Gerfen's expeditions into the unknown, and listen to their sound recording, by visiting the Myths, Ghosts & Legends website at www.spookythings.co.uk

Below: Even on a summer day one might feel the chill of the departed, watching from the shadows.

THE ANTIQUARIAN APPARITION

LOCATION: Bourne Mill, Farnham, Surrey, England

DATE: 2001

TESTIMONY: Jim Rice & Len Webb Witnesses

Bourne Mill is one of the oldest buildings in Surrey. It is situated on the edge of Farnham, which has long been reputed to be the most haunted town in the UK. The Mill is now filled to the brim with collectibles and antiques and is open to the public. Visitors come here to enjoy its ancient atmosphere, its excellent tearoom and, of course, its ghost. Sitting next to a large millpond beneath a canopy of lush trees, Bourne Mill is a mixture of red brick and weatherboarding and is a delight to behold. The building is mentioned in the Doomsday Book and the original millstone can still be seen, although nowadays it is used as a step, which leads to the pond. Antique dealers hire spaces in the many rooms of this building with its steep winding staircases and low ceilings. My story relates to the time when, along with my cousin and her husband, my wife and I operated Cousin's Collectibles at Bourne Mill. It was during this time that we caught a strange image, which seems to show the Mill's Phantom Lady.

We often took photographs of the items we restored, those for sale and the area from which we traded. On the occasion this particular photograph was taken, by my cousin's husband Len Webb, we were both present and it was one of several shots. We were not aware of any presence at the time. My cousin and her husband moved house some three or four years ago and as they were scaling down, and retiring from the business, they decide to throw out anything they no longer required, which included their photographs. It was only when my cousin was sorting through them that she realized that there appeared to be a woman in one of the prints.

When they first sent me the photograph I was convinced they were pulling my leg and asked how they did it, but I am now absolutely satisfied that it is genuine. We have had a few odd experiences at the Mill, particularly with the lamps that we had restored before EEC regulations required rewiring to be carried out by qualified electricians. On these occasions we would find, first thing in the morning, that standard and table lamps would have their shades tilted, dislodged or the entire lamp was lying on its side. It simply never occurred to us that it was anything other than visitors being disruptive, and I used to get quite annoyed. Strangely, nothing was ever damaged.

After conducting some research we found that the building is haunted by the ghost of a lady wearing a crinoline dress, who appears on a staircase.

Above: The village of Pluckley plays host to a plethora of paranormal happenings.

MOST HAUNTED?

LOCATION: Pluckley, Kent, England

DATE: April 2003

TESTIMONY: Paul Howse, The Ghost Research Foundation

This entry represents three firsts: my first investigation with the Ghost Research Foundation; a first for the GRF; and a first for any psychic research team in the UK: a chance to investigate Pluckley, which is 'Britain's most haunted village' according to the Guinness Book of Records (1997 edition), with its wealth of different ghosts that seem to almost outnumber the living. Pluckley has become famous for its spectral residents and has evolved into a Mecca for ghost hunters from around the world, much to the annoyance of many villagers. The Ghost Research Foundation was extremely lucky, therefore, to be the first research team to be officially allowed to conduct an investigation in the village.

Armed with an array of spook-hunting equipment, three mediums and high expectations, we converged at The Black Horse Inn, which lies in the centre of the village, on Saturday, 19 April 2003.

Above: The former site of Park Wood, on the edge of the village, is haunted by the ghost of a spectral Colonel.

Introduction

By around 6pm the entire 16-strong team had arrived and had a chance to get acquainted with each other. The team consisted of the following:

Diana Jarvis	*President and Medium*
Norie Miles	*Vice President*
Jason Karl	*Patron*
Veronica Charles	*Medium*
Andrew Garley	*Medium*
Paul Howse	*Senior Investigator*
James Lampert	*Investigator*
Bridget Lampert	*Investigator*
Andy Keast-Marriott	*Investigator*
Sian Rayner	*Investigator*
Paul Brown	*Investigator*
Elaine O'Regan	*Investigator*
Kevin Hough	*Investigator*
Wendy Craig	*Investigator*
John Mason	*Official Photographer*
Lyndi Telepneff	*Medium and Historian*
Dennis Chambers	*Pluckley Ghost Expert*

Once we had introduced ourselves to each other, mediums Diana Jarvis and Veronica Charles relayed their initial psychic feelings about the village. Before arriving Diana had seen a vision of a 'staircase' at The Dering Arms public house (where we were due the following day) and had also heard a 'rustle of silk' in her mind. She had also sensed the spirit of a small child inside The Black Horse, saying 'she is moving things, making things disappear'. This was very relevant as poltergeist behaviour has been reported as an ongoing phenomenon inside the building.

During the car journey, on the way to the village, Veronica, who had not been told where she was being taken, nor any of the history, had a vision of a 'Lady in Red', saying 'this Lady was a mistress and had some form of connection with jewellery'. This was very exciting as a Red Lady does indeed haunt the village. We were picking up strong emanations from the psychic world already, even on a car journey while hundreds of miles away.

Right: The investigators discovered a variety of different ghostly presences lurking around the Church of St Nicholas.

St Nicholas' Churchyard & Surrounding Area Investigation

Dowsing – Team One

Before we sat down to dinner at the inn, we took two separate walks in the surrounding area. In each case, members of the team used dowsing rods in an attempt to pick up any ghostly activity and to try and detect the presence of any ley lines. In each group there was at least one medium. As senior investigator, I accompanied both groups to record any findings. I did not pass any details of findings from the first group to the second because I was attempting to see if the groups would have similar results.

The first team, led by medium Diana Jarvis, began using dowsing rods outside the entrance to The Black Horse. The first intention was to see if we could find the ley lines and, if so, in what direction they ran. After some initial dowsing, it became very apparent that the rods, used by various investigators, were responding in a similar fashion. A very clear ley line was being indicated, running from the direction of the pub itself towards the school on the other side of the road.

We proceeded into the nearby churchyard. The entrance to the churchyard is not very wide and so the team entered one at a time. All three sets of dowsing rods crossed as they passed a particular headstone, just beyond the entrance. This was the headstone of one John Buss. The headstone was leaning back at a steep angle, and Diana picked up that someone 'wasn't happy about this' and that they wanted it to be straightened.

Diana then had another psychic sensation. She sensed people hidden in the church itself and this had a connection to war. Another member of the team, who has psychic abilities, picked up the name Freddy. This man had been followed or chased. He was aged between 67 and 70 and had long, uncut hair. He was bearded and had the look of a 'caretaker' about him.

Some of the group walked back towards the entrance to check on the anomaly with the rods by the headstone of John Buss. As they got to the entrance Bridget reported feeling sick and uncomfortable. This became worse the longer she stood at the entrance. Other members of the team also said that they, too, experienced strange feelings in the stomach while standing in the entrance. Diana noticed a definite 'change' in feeling as you crossed the threshold of the churchyard. I remarked at this stage that at a point on one side of the path a tap and on the other was a lamppost with power connections, directly in line with each other, and that maybe this was responsible for the feelings.

Further dowsing in the churchyard revealed that Wendy's rods crossed repeatedly by the headstone belonging to Sarah Anna, and also by the war memorial at the crossroads of the paths in front of the church. As the team returned towards the pub the same results with the dowsing rods occurred as we passed the school, once again indicating a ley line running between The Black Horse and the school. Andrew Garley was next to sense a lingering feeling from the past. He picked up a man in black clothes, possibly the uniform of a policeman. But this man had no hat. He sensed something around the head or neck, suggestive of a strangulation.

Some of what this first group had experienced made sense, as I knew the stories of the hauntings, but I did not reveal anything at this early stage – we were just getting started.

Minutes later Diana went into a trance state and seemed to make contact with someone. She used the following words to describe him: 'rogue', 'criminal', 'dark'. She said: 'He does not walk alone, and he is a liar.' She added: 'He doesn't understand why he shouldn't lie or do what he does. He is very intelligent, but has some form of "mental psychosis" and is a compulsive liar.' Then a phrase came into her psychic experience which did not appear to make sense at first, 'holed up', which was then corrected to two different meanings, 'holed up' and 'hold up'. This was definitely a highwayman. Diana said that there was some hidden gold, possibly in a tin box. She had a definite image of a box and a flintlock pistol imprinted upon her psyche. This ghostly character is a well-known figure in Pluckley and we were due to visit his haunting ground, known as Fright Corner, the following afternoon.

Andrew had been standing close by and now received more information about his earlier man in a black uniform. This information confirmed that it was not in fact a policeman but a vicar or priest who had chased someone from the churchyard.

The mediums needed to rest and the investigators, pleased with the results of the dowsing experiment, made their way back inside The Black Horse. They sent group two out to meet me. I was

eager to hear what they would find and see if any of the information would match that given by the first team.

Dowsing – Team Two

The second group, although covering the same area, took a slightly different route. The team was led by mediums Veronica Charles and Andrew Garley. Veronica walked straight up to a large tree in the garden of The Black Horse Inn. She felt that a strong telluric earth energy was surrounding the area, focusing on the tree itself. Andrew tested the area with a pair of dowsing rods and came to the same conclusion – the 'energy' was caused by the presence of a nearby ley lines.

Group two made its way from the grounds of The Black Horse into the graveyard, entering by the smaller side entrance. As Veronica crossed the boundary she stopped dead in her tracks and stared through the twilight at the far end of the graveyard. She then walked, with some speed, up to a pair of headstones belonging to Harriet Alice and Harry Rowe, both had died aged 71. There was a period of silence while Veronica tried to ascertain the importance of these particular stones, but nothing was forthcoming. After a few moments her attention was drawn back to the church building and we trudged through the crumbling headstones until we were standing, huddled, around a small wooden side door. Placing her hands upon the door Veronica said: 'There is a woman in red silk, she is a "well-to-do" lady, very well presented. The word "skulduggery" is associated with her family. Although her appearance is gracious and elegant, materialistic wealth is unimportant to her. She appears with dark hair and in her mid- to late thirties. She is wearing a bustle and has a very strong link to the church.'

I was madly noting down each detail with accuracy to ensure that this 'evidence' could be closely checked later. Veronica, now deep in a trance state, continued: 'She had suffered a great loss and is filled with a sense of longing sorrow. I can hear someone saying "have to be buried", "have to get rid of". The man speaking is named Jack, and he has concealed something within a wall. Deceit abounds here; there is also an extramarital affair which resulted in a miscarriage. The name Catherine or Katrina is ringing in my head, definitely a "k" sound at the beginning of the name.'

Remarkably, much of this made absolute sense with a phantasm which has haunted the graveyard for many years. The Red Lady as she is known is believed to be the wraith of an early member of the Dering family, who were lords of the manor of Pluckley for centuries. The ghost is said to wander among the gravestones at night, sobbing bitterly and mourning the loss of a child which was hastily buried in an unmarked grave, following a still birth or early death. Whether this was the result of nature taking its course or infanticide is unclear, but the story does fit in with the sensations Veronica experienced. The male voice of Jack talking about burial and 'getting rid' of something might have been referring to this unfortunate child. Could it have been buried in a wall rather than in the ground as Veronica had sensed? Whether the Red Lady was the wife of a Dering lord or a Dering daughter is speculation, as is her name. The family records do not indicate that such a gruesome event ever took place, but that is not surprising if it was 'hushed up' as Veronica felt. Interestingly, a note in the church record of 1723 says '32 maintenance orders existing in relation to Pluckley residents – mostly against fathers of illegitimate children', which indicates that extramarital affairs could have occurred in the village. It was, however, the last piece of evidence that I found most compelling in Veronica's 'vision'. But this was only discovered later, when ghost expert Dennis Chambers related a snippet of local

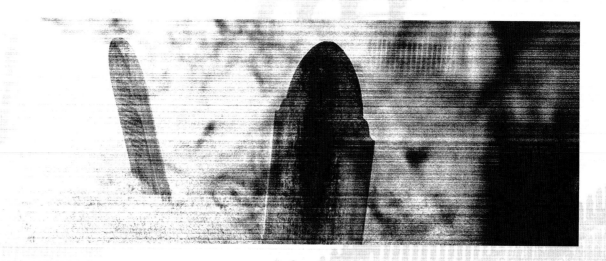

information which drew this story together. Veronica had been drawn to the tiny, apparently insignificant, side door in the church and had 'received' all her information while laying her hands upon it. I later discovered, from Dennis, that this door was once the private entrance door for members of the Dering family who rebuilt the church in 1475, naming it St Nicholas. The connection with the Dering's and the link with the Red Lady – allegedly a forgotten member of the same family – seemed, at least to me, quite remarkable evidence that Veronica had been in contact with the ghost of the Red Lady.

Sceptics would argue that Veronica had prior knowledge of the haunting, but I can say without a shadow of a doubt that having known her for several years, she cannot possibly have undertaken any research. She does not possess a computer and lives over 400 miles away from Pluckley. She did not even know where she was being taken when she got in the car to make the journey earlier in the day.

Following Veronica's revelations my attention turned to Andrew who was walking around the graveyard. He sensed a different spirit which, he claimed, was leaning on a headstone wearing a striped shirt with the sleeves rolled up. This spirit was smoking a pipe and looked about 45 years of age. When I examined the headstone it read George Winfred. Could this be a new ghost for the village? There have been other ghosts reported here, too. The first is that of a female figure in modern attire, but she has only been seen inside the church building, which at the time was locked. The second is a small white dog that runs among the pews before disappearing. During the 1970s, a group of ghost hunters convinced the Reverend John Pittock to lock them in the church all night to see if they could capture evidence of ghosts. They reported the next day that they had experienced nothing whatsoever of a paranormal nature and had found the entire night extremely dull. Their only respite was when the vicar's dog turned up to keep them company for a short while. The strange thing was that the vicar did not have a pet dog and no trace of any dog could be found.

There is a second haunting connected with the Dering family, which centres largely on the church itself, that of the White Lady. But our mediums had not been able to connect with this particular ghost. She is said to manifest in the Dering Chapel, emitting a white glow and wearing a sumptuous gown which glistens with spectral light. Legend has it that she died prematurely and was such a beauty that her bereft husband had her body interred inside seven lead coffins, one placed inside another, with a red rose upon her breast. The coffins were placed into an oak casket which was placed beneath the vault of the church. The caskets were thought to preserve her physical beauty for all time, while her non-physical spirit freely roams the building and among the gravestones. This same ghost also haunts the manor house of nearby Surrenden Dering, or at least the remains of it, for it was burned to the ground in 1952. It is said that an underground passage once linked the church and manor house and the White Lady still uses this tunnel to visit her old haunt. Evidence of the tunnel can be seen in the organ well, where a door leads to a bricked up passageway. Her form was seen gliding through the library of the former Surrenden mansion on at least one occasion, when a visitor tried to shoot her with a shotgun. The bullets lodged themselves firmly in the wooden panelling after going straight through the phantom figure.

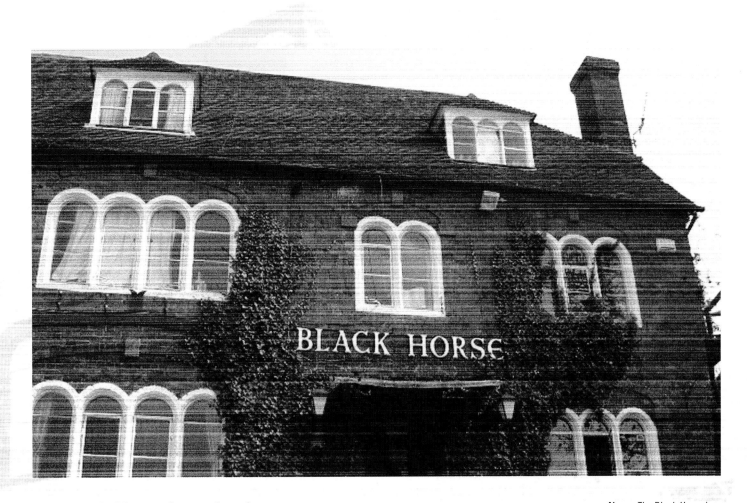

The Black Horse Investigation

By now it was getting dark and we decided to begin our preliminary investigation of The Black Horse, where we were staying throughout the coming night. I went with the mediums Diana Jarvis, Veronica Charles and Andrew Garley, along with investigator Andy Keast-Marriott around the building. Veronica was first to pick up a psychic sensation. She described a woman who was connected with the outside of the building, possibly the car park area. The woman had, according to Veronica, died from a collapsed chest and inability to breathe. The sound of screaming was ringing in her ears, as if some horrific accident was being replayed in her mind. I tried later to find out if such an incident had ever happened, but I was unable to verify the psychic vision.

Diana had been quiet while Veronica was talking, but now she had picked up on a spirit which she said 'moves fast'. The feeling of the entity was that it was moving through a wall in the main bar area where a large snooker table now stands. This was interesting as I later discovered that there had been a doorway in the wall, but it had been bricked up and plastered over some time ago.

We left the public areas and ascended the staircase. As we reached the top, Diana said that something was playing hide and seek with us. She described a mischievous, childish feeling associated with this psychic feeling. One of the ghosts at The Black Horse is known as the Poltergeist and is thought to be a ghostly prankster with benign intentions. The building dates back to 1450 and began its life as a moated bailiff's house, which was used to manage the Dering estate. It has been suggested that perhaps the spirit originates from this period prior to its use as a coaching inn. Landlords and staff have reported the disappearance of objects, including clothing, sometimes for long periods, which later reappear where you least expect. Former landlady Laura Gambling, who took up residence at the inn in 1997, was amazed when she watched a glass moving along a shelf one Sunday afternoon as she drank a cup of tea. The same ghost is blamed for setting cutlery on tables ready for customers to enjoy dinner in the dining room. On one occasion a full apparition, described as a 'nice lady in a red dress', was seen in an upper room. Could this have been the Poltergeist, or was this the Red Lady from the churchyard next door, visiting her spectral neighbour?

Above: The Black Horse is haunted by a playful poltergeist who, according to the investigation team, is the ghost of a young girl who fell to her death in a nearby barn.

The investigation group moved into the Shower Room, which is a large unused bedroom that houses a dilapidated shower in one corner. At once Andy registered a high electromagnetic energy reading with his Gauss meter. The strange thing was that this 'anomaly' seemed to be hovering in mid air. The readings above and below it and to either side showed nothing odd, yet a higher reading was recorded on the scientific equipment. It became apparent that the 'energy' was spherical in shape, but moments after this had been recorded it dissipated and could not be located again. If this had been a natural electromagnetic field it should have been constant, not dissipating, and certainly not hovering in mid air.

Based on this we decided to set up a trigger object in the room. We selected the shelves just adjacent to the area where the sphere of energy had been floating and there placed a key dusted with flour, so we could tell later if it had moved – even slightly. We also set up a 0-Lux camera to monitor the trigger object. This camera broadcast the image through a wireless video link to recording equipment, situated downstairs in the public area of the building.

During the excitement of the energy anomaly a special guest had arrived downstairs. Dennis Chambers, the undisputed authority on Pluckley's ghosts, had agreed to give us a talk on the village and its haunted heritage and we made our way downstairs to meet him.

Dennis Chambers' Presentation

Dennis very kindly rearranged his busy schedule to spend an hour or so with us, so that he could talk to us about his experiences of the ghosts of Pluckley and the information that he has collated over the many years he has been investigating the village's hauntings.

He first talked about the inconsistencies in the reported number of ghosts haunting Pluckley. Some report 12, some 13 and others say 16. This, of course, has an impact on Pluckley's status as 'most haunted village'. It is Dennis's opinion that some sightings of the same or similar events, over time, became individual ghosts, so adding to the number. The consensus from most sources agrees that the 'official' number of recorded ghosts is 12. Our research will point out, however, that this may not be the case.

Dennis talked for a short time about The Black Horse Inn. He told us that although ghostly events had been recorded there, he considered The Blacksmith's Arms as the more paranormally active hostelry. The Blacksmith's Arms, which we were due to visit the following day, was once named The Spectre's Arms after the alarming number of ghosts said to inhabit the building.

Dennis had been extremely friendly with the previous landlord of The Black Horse, Ted Kingston-Miles, who was licensee for almost 15 years. This was unusual, Dennis said, as landlords rarely stayed that long. Most only ran the pub for 12 months or so before they moved on. In fact, the landlord at the time of our visit, Nick Alvanos, was moving on in the near future. Dennis then told us of some of the reported haunted happenings that Ted had described to him over the years. These included a solid wood furniture suite being purchased and placed in the front bedroom, which after only a few hours had been damaged by some unseen force so that each leg had broken off – no one had entered the room during the time. Also reported were many instances of loss of property. Things being moved then reappearing days later in places that they could not have gone unnoticed before.

The Dering Arms, which we were due to investigate the following night, was next on Dennis's list. He informed us that there were lots of reports here from the 1980s onwards of a ghost of a little old lady who sits down at a table by a bay window. Apparently, she is so clear that many times she is taken for a real person. However, she wears an old-fashioned dress and bonnet, and as soon as her presence is commented on she inexplicably vanishes without a trace. We wondered if we might encounter this friendly spirit the following night.

Dennis continued relating his tales of the other ghosts in Pluckley, and we all listened intently as the talk began to centre on the church we had investigated earlier. If you will recall, Veronica Charles had placed her hands on a small wooden door at the rear of the church. While doing this she had picked up some extremely detailed information about the Red Lady. We were all surprised to find out from Dennis that there was a path that led from the Dering estate through the churchyard to this very door, which was once the Dering family's private entrance to the church and to the Dering Crypt. It seemed amazing that Veronica should pick this information up while in physical contact with the door, because at the time none of us had any prior knowledge of its significance.

Next we were told of the various cottages which had been destroyed by Doodlebug bombs during the war. One such cottage had stood very near to The Black Horse. We all stared at Veronica as we realized that her earlier experience of a woman who had the feeling of a weight on her chest, a crushing, and difficulty in breathing, might be explained in paranormal terms, by this historical fact.

Dennis concluded his talk by telling us about an interview that took place in 1985 with a man who had seen the Hanging Schoolmaster in broad daylight. This man had had no prior knowledge of the alleged ghost. We visited the site of this strange haunt much later in the evening and I shall relate my findings later in this case file.

With Dennis's knowledge firmly implanted in the team's minds we set about continuing our investigation of The Black Horse Inn. We climbed the staircase back to the Shower Room where we had discovered the anomalous electromagnetic energy sphere earlier in the evening. It was Andrew who next found a link to the spirit realms. He said that a young female child was standing behind him in the corner of the room, watching the team with great interest. He said: 'She has blonde hair and is the daughter of a servant who worked in this building before it was an inn. She was not allowed inside during her sentient life and she feels privileged to be able to come in here after death.' I asked him why she was haunting here and how she died, to which he replied on the ghost's behalf: 'She fell and broke her neck in a nearby barn after being told not to play there. She has a childish excitement about her, but it is suppressed by sadness – it is as if she was aware of the sadness her death caused to her mother on the earth plane, her mother is named Mary.' I wondered if she might be the cause of the poltergeist behaviour which has been reported for many years in the building. Moving items around could certainly be described as 'childish' and each incumbent of the inn has described the presence as 'playful'.

We were distracted from our communication with the young spirit by Andy Keast-Marriott who had been testing the area for electromagnetic energy fluctuations. He had found a high reading near to a wall just outside the room in which most of the group was standing. Strangely, as I walked towards him to note it on my paper pad, it dissipated and was gone. I immediately checked for any potential natural cause such as electrical wires in the wall or nearby energy sockets, but I found nothing. Had this been the electromagnetic manifestation of the young poltergeist with whom we had just been communicating?

We decided that we would explore the rest of the building for other signs of supernatural activity and we ascended the second staircase to the next floor. As we climbed Andrew noted a sensation which he said was caused by the presence of a woman wearing a flowing dress. This made sense, as another ghost, that of a 'nice lady in a red dress' had been noted in the past on the upper floors of the building. We entered every chamber in the building in our attempt to make contact once more with the Poltergeist, or indeed any other wandering wraith, but to no avail. For now, the ghosts had gone.

At the end of the exploration we arrived at a tiny wooden staircase which leads to the attic and the aptly named Hidden Room. Earlier in the evening Dennis had told us that in the past this had been the most supernaturally active part of the building, and we were hopeful that we might experience something of a ghostly nature as we ascended and made our way into the room in pairs. It is a dark and damp space devoid of light and filled with drifting cobwebs. A spooky scenario, but no activity was witnessed by anyone and we thought that perhaps it would be better if we came back later on, when the building was quieter. We made our way back down to the ground floor where there were still a few locals finishing their drinks and several wanting to ask us questions about our investigation. After they had left, leaving us alone in the haunted hostelry, Norie, one of the investigators, began a 'table tapping' session in the dining room.

To begin with nothing seemed to occur, but after a while our patience paid off as participants reported small movements and 'vibrations' which could be felt by those with their hands on the table. Some of the team were unable to take part due to spatial constraints and so they began their own session on a smaller table nearby. After almost an hour of tiny movements, but no 'tapping' we decided that as it was well past midnight, it was a suitable time to begin a spirit board experiment. We set up a Ouija board on a large table and began session one. The sitters were Andy Keast-Marriott, Paul Brown, Elaine O'Regan and Norie Miles. I recorded the session on a video camera. A transcript of the experiment follows:

Time: 2:20am

Norie: 'Is there anyone there?'
Nothing for several minutes

Norie: 'If there is anyone there could you please go to "yes".'

The Planchette very slowly moves around the board, picking up speed going down past the numbers and then circling. before finally moving to 'yes'.

Norie: 'Thank you. Could you please spell out your name?'
'C', 'O'

Norie: 'C O? Could you please spell out the rest of your name?'
No response
'O', 'K'

Norie: 'Is Cook your name?'
'NO'

Norie: 'Is cook your occupation?'
'YES'

Norie: 'Can you please tell us your name?'
'M', 'A', 'R', 'Y'

Norie: 'Is your name Mary?'
'YES'

Norie: 'Mary, did you used to live here?'
'YES'

Norie: 'Can you tell me what year it is?'
'1857'

Norie: '1857. Is that right Mary?'
'YES'

Norie: 'Are you married Mary?'
'NO'

Norie: 'Can you tell us your surname?'
'R', 'Y', 'D', 'F'
'NO'
The Planchette began sweeping the board in a circling fashion.

Norie: 'Is your surname Ryder?'
'YES'

Norie: 'Were you the Cook here, Mary Ryder?'
'NO'

Norie: 'Did you work here?'
'NO'

Norie: 'Did you live here?'
'YES'

Norie: 'Did you live here and cook for the other people who lived here?'
'NO'

Norie: 'Were you a Cook somewhere else Mary?'
'YES'

Paul takes up the questioning

Paul: 'Did you die here, Mary?'
'YES'

Paul: 'Did you have a happy life living here, Mary?'
'NO'

Paul: 'Are you happy where you are now?'
'YES'

Paul: 'Mary, do you have a message for anyone around this table?'
'A'

Paul: 'Mary is your message for someone who name begins with A? If it is please go to the "yes"'.
'YES'

Paul: 'Is the message for Andy?'
The planchette remained on 'yes'

Paul: 'Would you like to spell the message out for Andy? We thank you for doing this, Mary'.
'G', 'O', 'O', 'D', 'B', 'Y', 'E'

Paul: 'Mary, if you'd like to leave please confirm by going to "yes".'
'YES'

Paul: 'OK then thank you very much for communicating with us Mary.'

We closed the first session at 2.36am. After apparently communicating with Mary Ryder I remembered that the name had been mentioned earlier on in the investigation and checking back in my copious notes I found that Andrew Garley had said that the Poltergeist child's mother had been named Mary, and that she had lived in the building as a servant. The information gleaned from the session was beginning to make sense.

We held a second session and tried to re-contact Mary to ask some pertinent questions which would help us to identify her later. Andrew Garley replaced Norie and I took part as well, leaving the video camera recording what was happening. The answers were not as forthcoming and although we did seem to get some semblance of 'evidence' that we were communicating with Mary again, the energy was much weaker, and it was clear that we were not going to be able to continue for long. We did manage to ascertain that Mary wanted us to 'help' her in some way, although we were unable to understand what kind of help she required before the communication was lost. We were all tired and drained after the psychic experiments and several of the team decided to get some sleep in various parts of the building. As the strongest medium we asked Veronica to sleep in the Shower Room, the most haunted room, using an old pair of curtains for covers on a broken settee for a bed.

Dicky Buss's Lane

Norie, accompanied by Jason Karl and myself, thought it would be a good opportunity to visit the nearby Dicky Buss's Lane. It was quiet in the early hours of the morning and misty and chilly. It seemed perfect for our next ghost hunt, which was to find one of Pluckley's most famous spirits, the Hanging Schoolmaster.

We crept as quietly as we could along the road from The Black Horse until we were at the top of Dicky Buss's Lane. The story, retold many times, has it that in 1920 a Schoolmaster from the nearby village of Smarden would regularly meet up with Henry Turff, Pluckley school's headmaster. The two would enjoy a drink in The Black Horse while pondering philosophical questions. One summer the teacher from Smarden went missing and weeks later a local miller, Richard Buss, discovered a swinging body hanging from a tree. The body was identified as that of the schoolmaster from Smarden. He had committed suicide by hanging himself from a branch of a laurel tree which used to stand at the bottom of the lane.

As the wind whipped our coats and the mist hit our faces we descended into the darkened lane, which now leads to a few houses and a field gate. We were unable to see anything around us in the gloom of the overhanging trees and we did not encounter the spectral schoolmaster. The tree in which he met his end has long since been cut down and no traces of a swinging corpse could be seen. Many have dismissed this tale as legend, yet as we returned to The Black Horse, where the schoolmaster had enjoyed so many happy hours, I recalled that Dennis Chambers had told us of a report from 1985 in which the body had been clearly seen, swinging in the wind on Dicky Buss's Lane.

I was not yet ready to put an end to the night's investigations and so, accompanied by Andy Keast-Marriott, I made the decision to spend some time in the Hidden Room, where Dennis Chambers had told us that most of the ghostly activity was centred. Armed with video equipment which can record in the dark, we made our way up to the attic. The floorboards creaked beneath our feet as we crept through the silent inn. After spending an hour in the dusty chamber we had not experienced anything out of the ordinary and so we rejoined the rest of the team who were now fast asleep on various floors and chairs, many nestled up to the open fire for warmth through the night, which was unseasonably cold.

As I drifted off to sleep I wondered if we had come close to understanding who, or what, was haunting The Black Horse. The poltergeist activity had, it seemed to us, been caused by a young girl child who had broken her neck in a tragic accident nearby, and the 'nice lady' was her mother, a cook named Mary Ryder who had used a room here for lodging and yet worked elsewhere. Although it was by no means a complete picture, it will certainly add to the extended dossier of psychic research in Pluckley.

In the morning I arose to find that one of the barmaids, Natalie Russell, was cleaning the bar in preparation for a busy Sunday lunchtime. As the team were still dozing and not ready to leave I grasped the opportunity to conduct an interview with her and the chance to find out more information about the ghosts at the inn. She told me: 'There is a tale of a small girl aged between eight and nine who appears around the fireplace area of the dining room, she had lost her toys and is searching for them.' Our first confirmation that there was a ghost of a young female child haunting the building – this was our Poltergeist. I quizzed Natalie further, asking her what she had experienced herself. She described that a recurring haunting happens to people who stay in the front bedroom. Each night they are awoken at 3am for no apparent reason. On several occasions this had happened while Natalie was living in the building, although she had personally never slept in the room. Another member of staff, named Roy (who was currently using the room), had told her that he had awoken several times to see a young girl sitting on the end of the bed watching over him, and on one occasion she was accompanied by a second spectre – that of an older lady – possibly her mother, sitting with her. The most recent sighting of the little girl was experienced by Dave, the chef, who had seen her approximately 12 months ago, again in the front bedroom

On another occasion, in early 2003, Roy had been awoken by a blinding white light which had filled the room and lingered for several moments before shrinking to become a globe, then finally disappearing. Unfortunately, we were not able to investigate this room as Roy himself was in it asleep.

Next Natalie shared with me an incident when she had been in the corridor just outside her own bedroom, where there is a mirror in a recessed fireplace. While looking into the mirror she had seen 'something' behind her in her bedroom. A dark shape, a human form, she was unable to tell if it was male or female, but it moved across the room and when she turned to see it there was nothing there.

I asked her about the poltergeist activity and the mysterious disappearance and reappearance of objects throughout the building. Natalie said that during recent building works many items had gone missing and had yet to be found. When the workmen lifted the ancient floorboards they discovered a number of items which had gone missing over the previous months, including a hat, jumper, trousers and a pair of shoes, startling enough in itself, but made even more creepy by the fact that they were laid out to form the shape of a body. Another example of the playful poltergeist perhaps?

According to Natalie, who by now was looking distinctly nervous as we discussed the unseen beings that she shares her home with, it is not uncommon to find glass beer jugs flying off their hooks and smashing into pieces on the floor. One barmaid even watched as a glass hovered in midair before crashing to the ground.

I was about to conclude the interview but Natalie had one last anecdote to add to my notes. It happened to a regular customer when she used the ladies lavatory. She had been gone a long time and when a barmaid went to check on her they found her standing behind the door in a state of panic. She explained that she had been unable to open the door, as if something was pushing it from the other side. Later I examined the door in question and found that it moved with ease and did not stick or jam in any way. Perhaps the customer had been under the influence of spirits of a bottled kind, or maybe the Poltergeist was up to its tricks once more.

By now the entire team was wide awake and we packed up our ghost-hunting gadgets and thanked landlord Nick Alvanos for allowing us to conduct the first ever official investigation of The Black Horse. We made a short trip by car through the village until we came to The Dering Arms, which was to be our base for the rest of the Pluckley investigation.

The Dering Arms
We enjoyed a delicious lunch in The Dering Arms. As I sat in the bay window I wondered if I might catch a glimpse of the building's resident ghost, that of an old lady in a bonnet who is often seen sitting at the windows staring out onto the road. She has become 'part of the furniture' so to speak, her appearances apparently so frequent that little notice is taken of them. Who she is and why she remains here is unknown. As I glanced through my notes from the previous evening I noticed that Diana had mentioned a 'rustle of silk' and a 'staircase' connected with the haunting of The Dering Arms. This must surely have been a connection with the old lady, suggesting that perhaps she also walks the staircases here.

After lunch we set off on a trek around the village with the intention of visiting as many of the other haunted sites on foot as possible. I had planned a route and drawn a map to ensure we made the maximum use of the time. The team put on their walking boots. We retraced our steps back to the centre of the village and set off for the next haunted hot spot.

Having already investigated The Black Horse, St Nicholas's Church and Dicky Buss's Lane, our next port of call was the Old Bakery, a small house opposite The Black Bull. During some renovation work, which took place some years ago, the removal of an old Victorian fireplace sparked off some spectral intervention. Ghosts do not like disturbances and the footsteps and icy chill – felt even on hot summer days – were blamed on the presence of something from the spirit realm. While the road outside is said to be haunted by a coach and horses.

The story of the ghostly coach, which has been seen and heard trundling through the village on foggy nights, is one of Pluckley's most well-known ghost stories. It has been seen in a variety of locations throughout the village, and most often described as a coach with four horses. One notable sighting was made one October evening just after midnight by a local couple who had been babysitting their granddaughter. As they reached Pinnock Crossroads the road was blocked ahead of them by a coach in all its glory, with candlelight streaming from the windows as it made its way up the hill in front of them before vanishing into the mists. Another anecdote tells of a new villager who had no interest in, or knowledge of, the alleged ghosts of Pluckley. He was surprised when he saw a coach and horses pass right in front of him. Far form being 'ghostly' he simply accepted it as real, until he heard the tale of the ghost coach himself. A more recent encounter, in November 1997, involved the sound of hooves on a cobbled surface. The ghostly coach and four has also been heard swerving into a local hotel, before stopping and leaving an eerie silence in its wake.

Greystones

We walked down Station Road until we came across a large, pale-grey mansion on the left-hand side of the road in a leafy dell. This private house is called Greystones and is well known as a haunted house in the village. The current building dates from 1863, but it is thought that the tale of the tragic monk who haunts the grounds dates from an earlier building which stood on the site. This earlier building may have been connected to the church in some way, indeed, the current property was originally named Rectory Cottage until it was renamed Greystones in 1924.

The unwelcome resident here is the shade of a monk who it is believed conducted a love affair with the Lady of Rose Court (we shall meet her later). The pair where said to be deeply in love, but following her untimely death the monk sank into a brooding depression and eventually died brokenhearted. His ghost now wanders the grounds of Greystones, head hung in sorrow. This sad wraith was last seen by a visiting journalist in 1989, who clearly saw a figure dressed in a brown habit disappear among the trees at the back of the house.

As we left Greystones behind and continued our trek through this haunted hamlet, I wondered if any of the psychic members of the team would pick up on the next set of ghosts, that of a man and woman who can sometimes be heard chattering as they drift along Station Road unseen and accompanied by the sound of their yapping dog. But no mention of this gentle haunting was made and we continued on towards Rose Court.

Rose Court

At the corner of the road, which leads to Bethersden, we arrived outside Rose Court, which is a Tudor house inhabited by a female ghost. She has become known as the Lady of Rose Court, but her true identity is shrouded in mystery. Legend links her with the Monk of Greystones and she is said to have died staring out of a window which faces that house. It is also said that they were lovers in times long past and they shared many a secret rendezvous among the lanes and trees that surround their respective 'haunts'. Their relationship would not have been tolerated and the torment was said to have been too much for the lady, and she killed herself after drinking a poisonous potion of ivy and crushed berries. Another version of the same ghost story tells that the lady is the spectre of a former owner of the house who was the illicit mistress of a one-time Dering lord. In this version the house was built for the mistress by Lord Dering as a secret love nest. Her haunting activity is most prevalent between 4pm and 5pm, which was the time of day when she died. This mysterious ghost is also noted for haunting the gardens, and an eerie atmosphere is said to pervade them even on the sunniest of days.

The Brickworks

We continued down the road, leaving Rose Court behind us, and came to the Brickworks and our next haunting, that of the Screaming Man.

The tale of the Screaming Man involves a violent accident that occurred many years ago. An unfortunate worker fell headfirst into one of the clay-holes on the site, which have long since been filled in. The fear that he experienced as he fell has remained and his piercing scream of terror can still occasionally be heard, echoing around his former workplace. The mediums spent a few minutes in quiet contemplation with the genius loci, or 'spirit of the place', but no further evidence of the Screaming Man's spectral presence could be found and we continued on the tour.

The Watercress Lady

Reaching the Pinnock, we came to a small bridge known locally as Pinnock Bridge, which crosses a babbling brook. It is the haunt of Pluckley's next ghostly resident – the Watercress Lady.

Local folklore has it that in years past an eccentric gypsy spent her days here collecting the luscious watercress which grew beneath the bridge and sold it to villagers. The old hag was well known throughout Pluckley and despite her frightening appearance, meant no harm. Occasionally, she visited the village shop to buy a small bottle of gin, which would see her through the cold winter nights. This habit, however, was to bring her more warmth than she intended. One fateful evening after collecting watercress all day she was sitting on the bridge smoking her clay pipe and enjoying a tot of gin from her flask when she fell asleep without putting out her pipe. Minutes later she was engulfed in a fireball. A spark had set fire to her shawl which was sodden with splashes of gin. The screaming fiery figure battled with the flames before falling to the ground and burning to death. In the morning nothing but a few charred remains were to be found. The ghost of the Watercress Lady can still be glimpsed from time to time on Pinnock Bridge within a ball of flame, her screams piercing the darkness before all is silent and peace returns once more.

We sat for a few minutes on the side of the bridge, pondering the grisly demise of the harmless old gypsy and seeing if any of the psychic members of the team could pick up any trace of her presence, but it was not to be. Veronica felt she had passed on from this life many moons ago and that the haunting had 'worn down' over time. She was, indeed, correct because contemporary reports do indicate that the sighting has now diminished to merely that of a faint orange glow. The howling screams of pain are now heard no more. The Watercress Lady has at last found eternal rest.

The Ruined Windmill

Leaving Pinnock Bridge and the memory of its horrific haunting behind, we set off to try and locate the ruined windmill which was struck by lightning in 1939 and burned to the ground. The former miller, Richard Buss (also known as Dicky Buss), is thought to haunt the site and has been reported many times over the years as an ominous black figure lurking around the remains of the building. Unfortunately, we could find no trace of the former haunt and as the weather was good – his spirit is said to only appear before a storm breaks over the village – we decided to move on and try our luck elsewhere.

Fright Corner

We headed up the road towards the Screaming Woods (named after the inexplicable ghostly howls that are said to echo from the gloom of the forest), until we arrived at the crossroads known locally as Fright Corner. This is the haunting ground of the Highwayman, whom Diana sensed in the churchyard the previous evening. She described him as a rogue and compulsive liar and saw the image of a flintlock pistol imprinted upon her mind. The various elements of this psychic vision were consistent with the tale connected to this lonely spot on the edge of the village. The hidden box she had glimpsed in her vision may well contain loot stolen by this criminal.

There are many accounts of the phantom footpad being sighted here, most notably at the site of an old hollow oak tree which once stood at Fright Corner. The tale has it that in the eighteenth century a local brigand adopted Hothfield Common, near to Pluckley, as a killing ground for his villainous activities and accosted travellers making their way from Ashford to Maidstone. News of his activities eventually reached the authorities who dispatched a company of soldiers to deal with him. After being pursued through the village, the Highwayman made a dash for the woods. He dismounted and, assuming that his horse would canter off, he hid inside the ancient dead oak tree. His horse, however, instead of fleeing in fear began to graze and so indicated that its master was still around. A shrewd officer noticed the wooden hollow and running up to it thrust his sword into a hole in the trunk. As the blood of the Highwayman was spilt on the ground so a new haunting began.

There are no traces of the haunted oak tree left and yet you do not seem to need psychic abilities to feel the eerie melancholy of this quiet crossroads. We voted to leave this solemn place, and to bypass nearby Screaming Woods, and made our way towards the next haunted site – Elvey Farm.

Elvey Farm

The rambling farmhouse at Elvey Farm was built in 1430, but during the 1500s an upper floor was added and the building was converted into the farmhouse, and hotel, that stands today. The first reported sighting was a shining ball of white light, or orb, seen in February 1970 by a Mrs Ambrose, who ran a riding stables at the farm. She watched as it rose from the floor of her bedroom before floating across the room and disappearing into the chimney breast. A month later she had her second brush with the supernatural. At 8pm, as she was brushing her hair in front of a wardrobe mirror, she glanced over her shoulder and saw a young man with a short, fair beard, lying on the bed behind her. When she turned to look at him the bed was empty and the room was icy cold.

The next night her husband, who had not been told of the encounter, dreamt of a young man in a Victorian grey suit, who appeared next to the bed and was shaking violently as if suffering with a terrible fever. The dream disturbed his sleep and as he woke he had the distinct feeling that the front door had been unlocked. Sure enough when he ventured downstairs, the front door was wide open despite it having been locked earlier on in the evening. During a later discussion, it became apparent that the 'ghost' in the dream had the same appearance as the ghost in the mirror. Other visitors to Elvey Farm have been disturbed in the small hours by the sound of doors being opened and closed, while interference with the lights has also been blamed on the restless spirit that walks here.

Records indicate that during the 1850s a tenant farmer fell on unfortunate times and after his farm failed and his wife left him he shot himself in the old dairy building. It is said to be his ghost that walks at Elvey Farm, often accompanied by the strange, and confusing, scent of singed yarn or wool.

We were not due to spend the night at the farm and so continued on our 'haunted grand tour'. By now we were all thirsty and next up, fortunately, was a haunted pub.

The Blacksmith's Arms

The Blacksmith's Arms, formerly called The Spectre's Arms and The Ghost's Arms, is well known as a haunted building in the village and boasts of at least three phantasms. By now, word had spread around the village that the Ghost Research Foundation were 'in town', and we were not surprised when landlord and landlady Jim and Daphne Bere introduced themselves to us and began to tell us of their own supernatural encounters. They asked if we would like to investigate the private rooms on the upper floor where members of the public are not usually permitted. We, of course, were thrilled at the chance. Daphne told us about the building's three different ghosts: a Tudor maid; a man dressed in the clothes of a coachman, who has been glimpsed staring into the embers of the fireplace in the public lounge; and a lavishly dressed cavalier who wanders through the upstairs, private rooms – mostly favouring a bedroom which overlooks the road. It is this third spirit that is blamed for the incessant footsteps which are heard walking on the staircase and upstairs hallway in the dead of night.

The building dates back to the fourteenth century, when it housed the local blacksmith's forge. It became an alehouse in 1627 and remained a licensed premises until 1994 when Gloria Atkins turned it into a tearoom for a period. It is from this time that sightings of the maid ghost first occurred. She is dressed in clothing of the Tudor era and stands silently turning an invisible spit in the fireplace, much to the amazement of those who watch.

After Daphne had given us the details of what she already knew about the ghosts, she invited us upstairs. We decided that the mediums Veronica Charles and Diana Jarvis should lead the way. Diana was first to register a paranormal phenomenon, that of a ley line, which she discovered using her dowsing pendulum. When I later checked this it seemed that this was the same line that had been highlighted the day before, running near the churchyard.

Veronica linked with a spirit that was haunting the premises. She described a strong presence in the bathroom and became visibly affected by the experience. She became short of breath and was clearly having trouble breathing, so I decided to take her out of the room. She took a minute or two to calm down and regain her breath and then I asked her what she had felt. 'There is a man who is aged between 50 and 60 in that room. He is a wicked man, and there is a sense of violence and disorder with him.' After spending some time in the front bedroom, but failing to discover anything about the cavalier who allegedly haunts that part of the building, we returned downstairs to chat with Daphne once more, and to relate our psychic findings. She had remembered other tales while we had been investigating upstairs and which she now described. These included jugs on the bar swinging and banging on their own, and, in some cases, swinging so violently that they would come loose and smash on the bar. A more recent occurrence was the voice of a man that had been heard in the corridor that leads to the storeroom which used to be a kitchen. This voice would either say 'Hello', or laugh in a low, deep and hushed tone. This particular phenomenon had occurred three times during 2002, each time at approximately 1pm. Daphne told us that he sounded like a 'sly' man by the way that he had said 'hello' and laughed at her. On each occasion that this had occurred, she had been entirely alone in the building, so ruling out the possibility of a prank or some kind of sound displacement.

After our short investigation we took advantage of an excellent ale to quench our thirst and I asked if perhaps we could return in the future to conduct a full scale ghost hunt. Unfortunately, Jim and Daphne were selling up (as seems to be the trend for Pluckley publicans) and so a return visit would not be possible. In June 2005 the building closed and plans were put in place to demolish it, but fortunately these were rejected and the ghosts still have somewhere to haunt at the time of writing.

Lambden Cottage

Before making our way to the last stop on our tour, we made a quick detour into Lambden Road to visit Lambden Cottage. This house is haunted by a ghost described as that of an old lady most often seen sitting in an armchair.

Park Wood

The last haunting ground to visit was Park Wood or at least the land upon which Park Wood had once stood. This is the home of the Colonel. The trees that once provided shadow for the spectral Colonel's perambulations are long gone. They were cleared for agricultural land in 1965. According to the legend, an army colonel killed himself in the wood by stringing himself up from a tree branch. The reason why he did this, and his actual identity, have remained a mystery for many years and, indeed, sightings of his wandering spirit, which were once prevalent, are no more.

The team could not pick up any trace of the alleged haunting, not surprising in this barren landscape which was once lush woodland, and so with our tour of haunted Pluckley complete we made our way back to The Dering Arms. As we walked I related the tale of another haunted property in the village, that of a house of undisclosed identity in which there is the spirit of a mad man. A former resident of the house came into contact with this ghost after hearing footsteps in what he believed to be a deserted bedroom. After picking up a cricket bat he charged at the door to enter the room, believing a burglar to be present, but what he experienced on the other side of the door caused him to flee the cottage in terror. He was thrown onto the bed by an invisible assailant and crushed beneath a force so powerful he never felt content in the building again. He left Pluckley for good a short time afterwards. During a later visit to the village, he related the encounter to a shopkeeper who told him that the very same thing had occurred to a previous inhabitant of the same building, and that the ghost was that of one Billy Bandon, a local man who had gone insane in the bedroom and whose spirit remains there still.

We reached the The Dering Arms, which was originally a hunting lodge and was built in the 1840s. After settling in for the night we got chatting to some locals about the tales of the little old lady's ghost. She was described with much affection as a 'friendly spirit' and was clearly accepted here as part of the community. Perhaps we should not have been surprised by this for Pluckley is immersed in spectral heritage and acceptance of the unusual, the strange and the unexplained is normal in this haunted hamlet.

In conclusion, we had had a very interesting weekend's investigation, which, as usual, raised more questions than answers. I was sure we had made contact with the Poltergeist and her mother in The Black Horse and definitely the Red Lady in the churchyard of St Nicholas. As for Pluckley's other resident ghosts, which according to my count is now 28, some carry with them a fleeting sensation of melancholy, others have faded away, but all are most definitely part of the colourful tapestry of Pluckley's haunted past.

The Ghost Research Foundation is one of the UK's oldest ghost research organisations and was founded in Oxford in 1992 by Jason Karl and Daniel Holmes. Peter Underwood, King of Ghost Hunter's, is the patron and membership is by invitation only.

For further information on Pluckley visit http://www.pluckley.net/history/ghosts.htm

For more information on Spiritquest and the ghost photographs they caught at St Mary's Church, Pluckley, visit http://spiritquest.mysite.wanadoo-members.co.uk/

THE SPECTRE IN THE CHAPEL

LOCATION: Woodchester Mansion, Stroud, Gloucestershire, England

DATE: October 2005

TESTIMONY: Chris Howley, Gloucestershire Paranormal Research Group

Woodchester Mansion has been an ongoing investigation location for the Gloucestershire Paranormal Research Group for some time, but the most exciting investigation to date, during which we captured an apparition on CCTV, was spread over two nights, and began on 7 October 2005. The mansion, which lies deep in a secluded valley among woods just a few miles south of Stroud in Gloucestershire, has been described as one of the greatest achievements of nineteenth-century domestic architecture in England. Construction on this Gothic Revival pile began in the mid-1850s, although the work was never completed. Was it simply lack of funds that halted construction or something more sinister that made the builders down tools and leave?

The valley in which the mansion is situated originally belonged to the Ducie family in the eighteenth and early nineteenth centuries. They built a substantial Georgian house called Spring Park on the land. It was in November 1845 that the northern part of the estate was sold to William Leigh, who commissioned the architect Augustus Pugin to suggest alterations to the existing house. Pugin proposed that the original building be demolished to make way for his more extravagant Gothic Revival design, but when Leigh and Pugin fell out, partly over money, Leigh turned to the less expensive Charles Hansom of Bristol to undertake the project.

In 1852 Leigh commissioned Hansom to replace Spring Park with a new house. It was to be Benjamin Bucknall, an architect trained largely by the Hansom brothers, who would develop designs for the new house. Strongly influenced by the designs of the great Gothic Revivalist Eugene-Emmanuel Viollet Le Duc, Bucknall now had the golden opportunity to deploy the theories of his French mentor.

Construction of the mansion halted in 1866. With his health failing, and morale sapped by a series of deaths in his family, including his two daughters at the ages of 21 and 32, doctors warned William Leigh that he should not live on a site which was damp. He therefore remained in his cottage at the lip of the valley, where he died in 1873. After passing through the hands of Leigh's son, the mansion has had a varied life. It was let to a farmer in 1923 who kept cattle in the dining room. During the Second World War, the pupils of a Catholic school were evacuated from Birmingham to the mansion, and the Home Guard used the land for training purposes. Today, the building is owned by the National Trust and maintained by the Woodchester Mansion Trust.

In October 2005 a small group from our paranormal investigation team was invited down to the mansion to set up a ghost watch for a group of local artists. We set up our closed-circuit television system close to the chapel corridor, because we had been informed of recent ghostly activity in that area. While the artists walked around the mansion with National Trust event co-ordinator Wendy Milner, the rest of us set up in the cellar with our usual array of electromagnetic field meters, night-vision cameras and recording equipment. Initially, there was little of interest to report but later on that would change.

After a short while Wendy's group of artists rejoined us and we retired to the drawing room for a break. On review of the CCTV footage from this first vigil we appeared to have captured a hooded figure appearing very briefly in the chapel corridor. Our first reaction was that it could be stray torchlight from the group wandering around, so I spoke in depth with Trystan Swayle, a colleague who had been with the party walking around the mansion, to ascertain where they would have been at the time of the visual anomaly.

We concluded that the group could not have been in the area where the hooded figure had been caught. At this point we still only had the torchlight theory to explain it, but possibly someone else had been around at the time. Our next plan was to post the footage onto several websites and to ask for comments as we were due back to the mansion the following Friday and wanted as many options to discount as possible. As you will read later on the anomaly we caught was not torchlight, infrared light or car lights, which were all suggested as a potential cause.

The force of fear

The rest of the evening was fairly uneventful until 2am, when I had to supervise two investigators leaving. After closing the back door I walked up the corridor and as I turned to go towards the chapel, a stone was thrown at me. To the uninitiated this could have been quite frightening, but it is a phenomenon I have become accustomed to, especially inside haunted Woodchester Mansion. Moments later I was running down the corridor as fast as I could, compelled by some unseen force of fear, and fell onto the floor, blood pouring from a wounded knee. Shaken by the experience all I can remember was seeing the stone come at me, and then feeling an electric charge run through my body. I cannot remember starting to run, but I remember getting to the end of the corridor before being pushed over by an unseen force. We decided to end our vigil at 4am and left, somewhat spooked by the incident.

The following Friday, 14 October 2005, we returned to the mansion. We were hosting a group event and were accompanied by 30 investigators. The aim was to follow up our previous investigation and explore the further possibilities of what could have caused the hooded figure. First, we attempted to re-create the CCTV image with torchlight. Three of the group walked around the mansion with a variety of torches while other members sat in front of the monitor with a two-way radio guiding us. We flashed light at every window to try to get a light source on to the area in question, but to no avail. As hard as we tried we could not re-create the image of the hooded figure. We established that due to the radial spread of torchlight the torch would have had to be held very close to the area to create the same effect. Whether you believe it is a spirit or not, as a group we have no rational explanation for the video image.

The atmosphere in the mansion on the second vigil was definitely intense. It was almost as if something was watching us and biding its time. Several investigators did sense a tall man in the chapel area moving between us, but no visual evidence was caught.

After exhausting all possible avenues to explain the apparition on the tape, we believe it is a genuine spirit manifestation. The interesting point is that the figure appears to be quite tall and this tallies with evidence from mediums who have 'seen' a tall man in this area prior to the film being taken. There is definitely something strange happening at Woodchester Mansion and we plan to continue our investigations of the building.

For more information on the research conducted by Gloucestershire Paranormal Research Group, including the opportunity of watching the ghost caught on video at Woodchester Mansion, visit their website at www.gprg.co.uk

For more information about Andrew Mercer's ghost photograph and his investigations of Woodchester visit the website of the Institute of Paranormal Research at www.iopr.org.uk

Information on Woodchester Mansion and its hauntings can be found at www.woodchestermansion.org.uk

Above: Borley; the Ghost Hunter's 'Mecca', still maintains an atmosphere of haunted gloom despite the rectory being destroyed many years ago.

IN HARRY PRICE'S FOOTSTEPS

LOCATION: Borley Rectory, Borley, Suffolk, England

DATE: June 2003

TESTIMONY: Dean White, Ghost Hunter

Borley's rectory was undoubtedly the most haunted house in England in its time. The rectory was built in 1863 by Reverend Henry Dawson Ellis Bull who passed away in 1892. Following his death his son Reverend Harry Foster Bull took charge. It was around the turn of the twentieth century that members of the family began to experience sightings of a ghostly nun within the grounds. She was seen on several occasions by different family members and visitors.

Successive rectors were witness to strange goings on at the rectory and in its grounds. In 1929 the then rector decided to call in some professional help and asked Harry Price, who became one of the world's greatest ghost hunters and psychical researchers of all time, to investigate.

Harry Price made his name in the psychic research field by writing and publishing several books and articles about the Borley hauntings, many of which were criticized by his peers. The haunting of Borley continued until the 27 February 1939 when the rectory was destroyed by fire. Arson was suspected but never proved and the ghosts apparently moved across the road into the church, finding a new haunting ground where sightings continue to this day.

Shortly after the fire at the rectory there was an excavation in part of the cellar where the skeletal remains of a young woman were unearthed, giving some credence to the legend of the ghostly nun. Later the burnt out shell of the rectory was levelled, and several bungalows were built. Even though the rectory no longer stands the ghost stories still continue.

Borley's church has a long history of haunting tales. One is of the church bell ringing by itself, while another is of phantom organ music playing from within the locked and darkened building. Investigations of the paranormal activity inside and surrounding the church have taken place since the 1970s and continue to the present day. One team of investigators managed to record noises emanating from within the deserted church, including tapping and the sound of a chair moving.

I have been actively investigating the unexplained for the last ten years after becoming a member of the Ghost Club of London. I read about Borley for the first time many years ago and it has always had a special fascination for me. Even though the rectory is long gone, the atmosphere of the haunted village still delivers a chill up the spine. There have been many books published on the hauntings at

Borley and the most recent contemporary work is Borley Rectory – The Final Analysis by Edward Babbs.

After reading this book I decided to make the journey to Suffolk myself and visit the village which had so often occupied my thoughts. On my first attempt I was unsuccessful, there are no road signs to Borley and locals will not offer directions if you ask. Only if you are lucky enough to stumble upon it will you find the the tiny village of Borley.

The mass media onslaught that has drawn thousands to the village over the last 50 years, fuelled by a ghost story that refuses to go away, is an unwanted intrusion to those that live here. Villagers have had enough of people turning up in the dead of night running about in the graveyard and making a nuisance of themselves. Vandalism to the church and roaring car engines in the small hours have added to the disharmony felt between Borley residents and those seeking a ghostly thrill without any thought for those who live here.

After several months of research I decided to make a second attempt at visiting the village of ghosts. This time I was accompanied by my friend Andy. When we realized that we had stumbled upon

Below: Borley Rectory was dubbed 'the most haunted house in Britain' by Ghost Hunter extraordinaire, Harry Price.

Below: Ghost Hunter Harry Price conducted a long-term investigation into the hauntings at Borley, and wrote several books on the results.

Opposite, top left: Inexplicable messages appealing for 'light mass' appeared inside the rectory.

Opposite, top right: The drawing room at Borley Rectory, during its haunted heyday.

Opposite below: This strange image appears to show a necktie hovering in mid-air behind the church at Borley.

the village, purely by chance, I was thrilled to be finally standing near to the site of what was once the most haunted house in England. The church is usually kept locked in order to deter troublemakers and vandals, but I had tracked someone down who had agreed to show me around. As I entered the church I walked right through an icy patch of air which was decidedly chillier than the surrounding air – was this a Borley ghost? After inspecting the Waldegrave tomb and taking some pictures of the famously haunted church, I returned to the grounds and began using my camera. I wanted to capture as much of the village, church and grounds as possible on photograph so that I could relive my visit later, and in case there was anything around which was invisible to the human eye, but which might be picked up by a lens.

After leaving Borley far behind and making the trek home I sent my pictures to be developed, not really expecting that I would see anything other than the church and landscapes which I had carefully composed, but to my amazement something strange was caught on film.

In the lower corner of a window of the church an indistinct face could be seen staring out. I sent the image to Tom Perrott, a long-standing member of the Ghost Club whose opinion on all things ghostly is highly regarded. He said that the picture was certainly interesting, and the writer Edward Babbs also agreed that it was of great interest. I will leave the reader to make up their own mind. For many, however, this could be the newest evidence of a haunting at Borley. I did go back to Borley several months later and took a second picture in the same window, using the same camera at the same time of day, but this time the face was not there.

Above right: Joanne receives a message from a former maid, in the shape of her image, via a printing machine at Hobs Reprographics in Coventry.

Opposite: The unexplained print which came out of the printing machine, of its own volition.

GHOST IN THE MACHINE

LOCATION: Hobs Reprographics, Coventry, England

TIME: February 2004

TESTIMONY: Joanne Gailey, Witness

My workplace is an old Victorian property and many of the staff here have had encounters with the resident ghost. The descriptions given seem to imply that it is the spirit of a maid because we sometimes also smell food cooking even though we have no kitchen. There is also a strange frightening atmosphere in the cellar and the odour of sulphur which we cannot account for. The experiences generally involve seeing the spirit in the peripheral vision, but in February 2004 another ghost made herself known in a much more dramatic fashion.

One of my colleagues was about to send a file to a printer and he decided to check if there was enough paper in the machine before he pressed the 'print' button. As he was checking the paper tray the machine whirred into action and it printed out an A3 image of the lower half of a lady in a long dress standing next to a table. We checked around the office that no one had sent this peculiar image to the printer, but no one had. It seemed to come from nowhere.

The 'haunted printer' became a topic of much conversation in the office and so I decided to conduct some research. An elderly gentleman customer, who often uses our services, was able to furnish me with some details about the building's past. He told me that in the late 1800s the property was a gentleman's residence and employed a staff of servants, and later in the 1930s it was used as a doctor's surgery. Unfortunately, he had no idea why there is a blocked off chamber in the cellar. An arched doorway can be seen behind a series of shelves which have now been attached to the wall. I wanted to find out more and so accompanied by a colleague we set off with a torch and found a small air brick in the exterior wall. Peering through the small gap we wondered if we might see something looking back at us, but the room was full of rubble and we left as puzzled as we began.

At first glance we wondered if the image which came out of the printer was that of the maid ghost, but upon reflection it seems to be of a more stately appearance, possibly a former lady of the house. Either way it is inexplicable and chilling to look at.

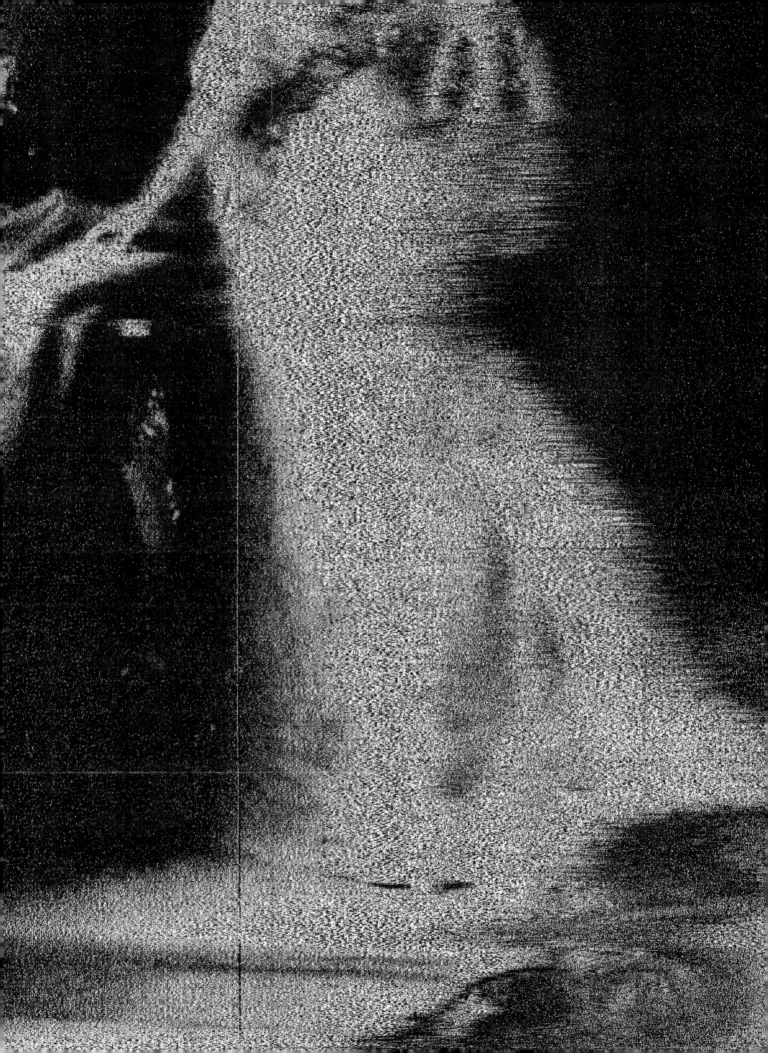

THE PHANTOM HITCHHIKER

LOCATION: Bridgnorth, Shropshire, England

DATE: October 2000

TESTIMONY: Andrew Homer, Association for the Scientific Study of Anomalous Phenomena / Parasearch

Coach driver Stuart Garlick had an experience he will never forget the night he stopped to help a stranded motorist. It was a dark night in October 2000 and he was taking a group of passengers to the picturesque country town of Bridgnorth in Shropshire. After picking up from various locations in the Dudley area he headed out towards Bridgnorth. Stuart recalls that he saw nothing unusual on that outward journey on the B1476 past Wombourne, and along the A454 Wolverhampton to Bridgnorth road. The passengers were going to spend some time in the town having a meal and a drink. Stuart decided to return to Dudley and pick the passengers up later that night rather than park up the coach and wait.

He returned the same way back along the Wolverhampton to Bridgnorth road. By around 8.30pm he was just passing through Worfield, about five miles from Bridgnorth. Caught in the headlights of the coach, Stuart suddenly spotted a hitchhiker. It was a man carrying a petrol can and Stuart's immediate thought was that he had broken down somewhere. He stopped to offer the hitchhiker a lift and the man got in the coach and sat down on the courier seat. The coach was in darkness with all of the lights out but even so, Stuart could see that his companion's dress was not quite as it should be. Stuart recalls that, 'he was dressed as though he had come straight from a 1960s or 1970s revival night, which I thought was rather odd. He had a wide lapel shirt, bell-bottomed trousers and an ear length "George Best" style of haircut. Just the sort of thing you would expect for a 60s or 70s disco night.'

The stranger talked quite freely. He had been on his way back from work and he said he had run out of petrol on his way home to Telford. This would have taken him along the B1476, known locally as 'the rabbit run'. He was rather appreciative that I should stop and give him a lift, remembered Stuart.

'We got to the island where you can go straight on for Wolverhampton, turn off left for Telford or turn right for Wombourne. There is a big pub there on the corner. I asked him which way he was going as I was only really killing time and I said I'd drop him off at his car. He said that the car was off towards Wombourne parked on the verge. I'd got to go that way anyway so we proceeded up towards Tinker's Castle and sure enough, there on the right hand side of the road, on the grass verge was a rather nice looking Triumph TR7 sports car. My passenger said it was a TR8 and that it was pretty rare. I thought it

was a TR7 but he was adamant it was a TR8. He also said that the car was a one off and was his absolute pride and joy. This was right on the crossroads at Tinkers Castle. So I pulled up more or less alongside the car, perhaps a little bit in front. He thanked me for giving him a lift, and said it would have taken him ages to walk the distance.'

'He got off the coach, thanked me again, walked past the windscreen in front of me, waved and disappeared out of sight. Whilst pulling off I then glanced in the offside mirror and he'd gone, completely disappeared! I first thought it might have been a blind spot. With any heavy goods or large vehicle there is a blind spot so I stopped and stuck my head right out of the window bearing in mind I'd only travelled a matter of a couple of yards. The road was straight so there wasn't a curve to obscure my view and he had definitely gone! I couldn't believe it. I looked right out of the window and there was nobody there on the crossroads. It was totally deserted. Not only that but the sports car had completely and silently vanished as well!'

'In the space of about 10 to 15 seconds he had got to get off the coach, walk around the front, cross the road (it was very quiet), open his fuel cap, pour the petrol in, fasten it back, get in his car, turn the engine over to pump the petrol through and then drive off. All of this in about 10 to 15 seconds and with no sound of an engine starting! Well, I can tell you, the hairs on the back of my neck stood on end, I just couldn't believe it. I tried to get away as fast as I could, I was crashing the gears. I just couldn't get away from the area quick enough.'

Who was he and where did he go?

To all intents and purposes the experience that Stuart had was very real. He even remembered getting a whiff of petrol from the can. The hitchhiker's conversation was normal and intelligent. However, in retrospect he did not seem to know the area very well and he was not sure how far or how long he had been walking. Stuart is also convinced that if the car had been there when he drove past on the way to Bridgnorth only half an hour before, he would have seen it.

The hitchhiker had a very long walk from the petrol station through the Shropshire countryside. It is a distance of about five miles from Worfield where Stuart picked him up, to Tinker's Castle where he dropped him off. The petrol station at Worfield was the only one in the area for miles around. At the time, Stuart was so bemused he decided to contact Worfield garage and find out who was on the till that night if only to reassure himself that someone else had witnessed the strange hitchhiker. The staff at the garage explained that the location is very remote and vulnerable and Stuart was told, 'We don't open for petrol here any more at night and haven't done so for many years.'

Andrew Homer is a paranormal investigator for ASSAP – www.assap.org, for whom he investigated this case, he also has his own group called Parasearch – www.parasearch.org.uk

HOUSE OF HELL

LOCATION: Raby's Farm, Lancashire, England

DATE: March 2003

TESTIMONY: Angela Borrows, Witness and Medium

In March 2003 I exchanged contracts on the purchase of a beautiful former farmhouse in the village of Catforth, Lancashire. Dating back to 1650, the one time thatched longhouse has seen many changes and alterations over its 350-year history. It also has two ghosts which I did not bargain on being included in the purchase of my new home.

The building today sits amidst acres of landscaped gardens and pastures and has been renovated over the last three years by myself with a lot of help from friends and family. After realizing it was haunted some time ago, I have never fully moved into the property, sleeping over only when I have been accompanied by friends or relatives, and with my dog Tee Tee, who appears not to be bothered by the ethereal presences.

The house was built in the first half of the seventeenth century as an agricultural farmhouse and was inhabited by John and Ellen Bolton. After the widowed Ellen passed away in 1658 she bequeathed the homestead to the Charities Trust, who used it firstly as a poor house and later as a meeting house where the board of trustees would discuss their business.

The trustees included several dignitaries from the surrounding area including Thomas Shaw, a surgeon from Kirkham, Reverend Wilfred Speakman and a solicitor from Treales. Records of the full names of the board are scant but they are thought to have included five men and one lady. The acreage of the farm was tenanted and the building and its lands were collectively known as Raby's Farm or Ray's Farm, although the origin of this name remains unclear. It is known, from minutes of the meetings held here, that loans were given by the Trust to local farmers and workers, with the paperwork being prepared at Raby's Farm. This was all part of the Trust's mission to help support the local people, infrastructure and agriculture.

In 1903 ownership of the farmhouse passed from the Trust into the hands of a private owner, and subsequently in 1956 it changed hands once more. The vendor from whom I purchased the house acquired it in 1976, and sold it to me in 2003, by which time it was in need of complete renovation and modernization.

I had an inkling it was haunted when I first stepped into it. It had that strange feeling as if you are not alone, but it wasn't in any way disconcerting. In fact, it made it rather appealing to me as I work part

time as a spirit medium. At the end of my fourth viewing I asked the vendor if it was haunted. She told me that on many occasions she had sensed that she was not alone in the room known as the lobby, although her husband refused to comment but gave me a wry smile. I was sold on it now for sure, and after the sale was completed I was looking forward to bringing it back to its former glory and moving in.

A figment of the imagination?

The first job was clearing the gardens, fields and various outbuildings, and together with a group of friends the work began in earnest. It was one lunchtime about two weeks after I had taken possession of the property that I was to have my first brush with the supernatural here. It was a bright Saturday afternoon and I was working in the garage. I needed to switch off the electricity mains and so I went into the house and into the utility room where the mains switch is located. After I had switched it to the off position I turned around and made my way through the lobby towards the kitchen, but something caught my eye and I looked down the long corridor which runs the entire length of the house and saw a figure staring out of the middle window into the gardens where I was working with a friend. She was totally static and as I watched, amazed by what I was seeing, my heart began to thump in my chest. Who was she? She was wearing a long black dress and had a pale complexion. Her hair was twisted into a bun and she stood motionless as I watched her, before suddenly disappearing – causing me to question whether I had seen her at all. My first reaction was to dismiss it and just consider that I must have been imagining things, but later that evening as I lay in bed I could not shift the image of the woman in black from my mind. I had not yet moved into the house, having decided to carry out the major renovation work first, but now I wondered what else might occur in my new home.

I moved into Raby's Farm on the 1 May 2003, but often slept at my other property as I felt uncomfortable being alone inside the farmhouse at night. I had been spooked by the sighting of the mysterious woman and wanted confirmation that what I had seen was not merely my imagination, caused by tiredness and the stress of moving and the renovations. To this end I contacted a magazine and asked if they could send in a psychic to investigate further. At the end of the psychic's visit she concluded that the house was haunted by a woman whom she had seen in one of the rooms. From the description it sounded like the same ghost I had seen, but on this occasion she was wearing a red dress rather than a black one.

This first experience with the phantom lady was nothing compared to what happened later when a friend named John Riley visited on the 5 June 2003. John is a sensitive and spends much of his time visiting haunted locations for various study organizations. He is used to sensing spirits and I wondered if he would pick up on my lady ghost.

As soon as he stepped into the house he said there was a priest in the house. I was surprised as I expected him to pick up on the lady – this was a new ghost to me. We had planned to go out for dinner

and when we made our way back to the house later that night, the atmosphere had changed in the house. As we sat in the lounge, John tried to 'tune in' to anything that might be present. I decided to take some photographs and was amazed at the results. As John sits in the armchair trying to link into the spirit of the house, an amorphous ball of orange light can be seen floating above his head. It is surrounded by a foggy mist in which several globes of white light are hovering. Strangest of all, several fronds of blue ectoplasm can be seen emanating from the ball of light. This is one of the strangest pictures I have ever seen.

After the excitement of the first photograph, John was keen to see if we could catch anything else on film and so the next morning he set about taking as many pictures as he could. It was 11.30am when he began taking snaps of the lounge, where last night the ghostly energies had been caught. After taking an entire digital data card of images we downloaded them to my computer to examine them – and were amazed at what we saw.

Amidst a set of images taken in succession was a picture of my French windows in the lounge and there was a man standing outside looking in, but he had not been there when John took the photographs. We examined the picture in detail, blowing up the various sections of the picture, and there as clear as day is a figure of a man wearing a dark grey suit, yellow cravat and white shirt. His face is partially obliterated by a glowing white light and the bottom half of his body cannot be seen as I had placed my garden chairs up against the windows the night before. We know he was not a real person as the house is quite remote and callers do not visit unless it is arranged – after all I am not here most of the time.

I was unnerved by the image and John felt that he was the man that he had sensed the evening before – the priest. I wanted to check whether there was any mention of priests in the deed of the building and after searching I discovered a paragraph which makes two references to Quakers having a connection to the house. Was this our ghost, a Quaker priest?

The picture was undisputable proof that the house was haunted. It was as if the priest had come inside and was making me nervous in my own home. Indeed, I never felt alone whichever room I went

into – unseen eyes were observing me wherever I went. Footsteps would be heard in deserted rooms and door latches would rattle of their own accord. One evening, while preparing for a dinner party someone called 'Hello Love' in a deep gravely voice into my ear. Something had changed in the house, it had turned darker.

Over the proceeding months it became a power struggle between my mind against the ghost of the priest. I sensed that he felt I was intruding in 'his' house. The name William kept ringing in my mind and when I checked the historical records the name came up time and time again. One evening I decided to sit down and try and communicate with this unwanted spectral visitor. As I cleared my mind, visions and thoughts from William flooded in. He was a lady's man and was used to getting his own way. In his time women had been submissive and that was why we were at loggerheads. I am not a submissive lady. In my mind's eye I saw him as a debonair kind of man, a dapper character who lived off his charm and wit. A sense of arrogance and self-importance filled my body. After sensing his personality I realized that we would simply have to try and live with each other, but in all honesty I hated sleeping there alone, and as each night beckoned I wondered what the hours of darkness might bring.

Several visitors have seen him in recent months, once standing in the lobby doorway and on other occasions walking past the windows outside. I decided a while back that I could not share my home with this domineering ghost and so once the renovations were fully completed I put it up for sale.

For me Raby's Farm represented the country home I always wanted, but as I have learnt you do not always get what you bargained for, and the power of the spirit world can literally rock your world so much that in the end the only answer is to admit defeat and move away. I will be glad to leave my house of hell when I finally exchange contracts, and I hope that when I leave, the ghost of William will do too. May he rest in peace.

Above: Mains Hall, Lancashire's most haunted house, is home to a friendly spectre named Lily.

LILY'S STORY

LOCATION: Mains Hall, Singleton, Lancashire, England

DATE: 1991 - Present

TESTIMONY: Adele Yeomans, Tarot Consultant

Tucked away in a suburb of Blackpool is the historic village of Singleton. Its origins date back to the medieval period. My story begins about 15 years ago, when my husband bought the listed manor house known as Mains Hall. The manor is on an estate which dates back to at least the thirteenth century and was built upon crossed ley lines. Within its antique walls is a wealth of history and it can even boast a royal intrigue during the Georgian period. According to historic sources, the very beautiful and scandalous Maria Fitzherbert was visited by the Prince of Wales, later to become George IV, when her family, the Fitzherbert-Brockholes, lived here. Many other famous local families have resided here, but the house has been dominated for over 300 years by the Heskeths of Maynes who were related to the Heskeths of Rufford Old Hall.

During the first ten years or so, Mains Hall was run as a country house hotel and regular sightings of ghostly phenomena were reported to staff by guests. The staff, too, told of experiencing strange events in all areas of the building and some were afraid to lock up late at night on their own. There are numerous stories I could relate of the spectral visitors we have seen here. Some seem to return again and again, perhaps reliving some past event whether it was a disturbing event that left them unsettled or something happy, recalling joyous times they had when they were alive here. Other ghostly encounters may be a psychic imprint on this ancient building, rather like a video recording playing back over and over again. One sometimes wonders if these spectral visitors are more put out by our presence in 'their home' than we are of them.

Cavalier types have been sighted in the old winter snug and have been seen by at least 12 people at one time. One poor wretch has been seen fencing some invisible foe on the stairs. Nannies are seen patrolling the corridors, perhaps searching for the children who used to live in the west wing where the nursery was during Victorian times. Children also feature strongly in one area of the hall and often visitors say they feel the chilling fingers of little ones clutching desperately at their hands, perhaps seeking comfort and reassurance from sympathetic adults. Are these the Hesketh children, some of whom sadly died at a tender age, as was so often the case in those times? A dark, hooded figure is seen silently drifting behind the back stairs where priest holes have been recently uncovered. It is a well-known fact that Cardinal William Allen, founder of the College of Douai, sought refuge here during the

time his brother-in-law, William Hesketh, was a tenant here in the mid-1500s. Could the hooded figure be the cardinal returning to his favourite hiding place? Some people have seen a royal visitor and his elegant lady in various rooms which were once her drawing rooms. As one source puts it: 'The best in the land have trod these boards!' Maybe in some twilight zone they still do.

Centuries ago it is believed that Mains Hall was home to tenant lay brothers from Cockersand Abbey until the Dissolution of the Monasteries between 1536 and 1540. Legend speaks of 12 monks who, having died of the plague, were buried beneath ancient trees overlooking the river. Misty forms have been seen by many of what look like monks in robes going about their business in the grounds of the estate. Tales of underground tunnels leading from the Hall have fuelled many a debate as to whether these were used by persecuted priests or by smugglers. Long ago smugglers would row quietly up the river under cover of darkness to hide their contraband. Shapes are seen frequently down one corridor where, allegedly, the tunnels begin. Did some poor unfortunate lose his life in these tunnels?

Among the many tales of spectral monks and ghostly smugglers, one fascinating story centres on a time much closer to our own, or so I believe. When telling stories about ghosts, people find them either incredulous or intriguing. I hope you find this one the latter – I certainly did.

Even though we were the owners we did not live on site in those days when it was a fine country house hotel, until fate triggered a series of events which were to change our lives considerably. In December 2001, following a small fire in the kitchen area, we, as a family, decided to move back into the hall while extensive renovations were carried out, intending to reopen for the Christmas period. Those first few weeks were stressful as the builders took over and began their work. This was when things began to get really interesting from my perspective. My husband and I moved into what used to be Room 4, which overlooks the beautiful River Wyre and had been a favourite 'haunt' of the smugglers and monks. This room was often the subject of much debate among the staff, as some felt decidedly uncomfortable whenever entering this beautifully furnished room. Guests often complained the next morning of having been disturbed throughout the night. Some reported a child sitting on the bed, others spoke of a male presence which seemed to unnerve them. No one, however, had mentioned what I was to encounter.

Right from the start, sleeping together with our dog Kara, a huge Weimeraner, I experienced some very disturbing dreams or visions. I would be awoken at some ungodly hour in the early morning, cold and terrified after having had a fitful sleep of nightmarish scenes featuring a woman and a dead baby. Upon awakening I felt a presence standing very close to my bed. Kara picked up on this because she would let out a soft growl. She at first slept on the bed with us, but she too would never settle and would wake up, pace the floor and stare out of a particular window. I decided to put a stop to her sleeping with us, feeling that perhaps it was her that was disturbing me. However, the visions were always the same – I saw a woman dressed in dark clothing, black or navy, with a small neat white collar around the neckline of her dress. Her hair was slicked back, dark and she had pale skin and red lips. The dress looked either late Victorian or like a three-quarter length evening dress one would wear even today. She always looked so sad and melancholic but she said nothing – thank goodness, or I fear I would have jumped right out of my skin there and then. Every time these visitations happened I would wake my husband to ask 'did you hear anything, see anything?' 'No,' was always the answer, 'I was asleep!'

I was more intrigued than terrified by these nightly events and felt that this lady was here for a very good reason. Why was she so melancholy? I wondered if I could discover the reason. Eventually, some of the fire damaged rooms were finished and much of the original timber frame of the building was uncovered, which we carefully restored. Thanks to a series of more fateful events in our lives we began to re-evaluate whether or not we should move in permanently to the hall and continue with the restoration.

As the refurbishment of another bedroom was finished we moved out of Room 4, which I was thankful for, because the disturbance of my sleep was beginning to take its toll on me. I was exhausted most mornings. Our new bedroom was lovely and housed a four-poster bed. This room overlooked the

front of the property and for a while everything seemed quiet. One morning, as I left my bedroom and descended the stairs, I noticed out of the corner of my eye a figure in black just outside Room 4. I quickly turned around only to discover that there was no one there. I called out 'Hello? Beccy?' thinking it may have been my daughter who was living in the attic part at the end of this corridor. No reply. I hesitated outside Room 4. It had been some time since any of us had been in this room and we had not started to renovate this part of the house. Nervously, I opened the door and for a fleeting second saw the misty shape of 'my lady' looking out towards the river, then she vanished. It took all of my courage not to slam the door and run, but I steeled myself and stepped in. I stood in exactly the same spot as she had and it felt so cold the hairs stood up on my arms and the back of my neck. 'Hello friend, I'm here,' I said, not knowing what to expect. Can ghosts speak? Silence. I stayed a few more minutes in the room and then left, quietly shutting the door and saying as I went, 'Goodbye'.

I did not see 'my lady' every morning, perhaps I was too busy, distracted or not as aware as usual, but as time went on this morning meeting became so normal I began to call out 'Morning!', just as I would when meeting anyone else. As the days went by I began to feel a strong link to her, even coming up with a name which continually popped into my head each time I saw her – Lily. My morning greeting became, 'Morning Lily, how are you today?' Of course she never replied, but I feel we had struck up a friendship of sorts. She was usually there most mornings and I felt that somehow she was making an effort to be there. I even lit a candle and put a vase of lilies at the top of the staircase in her honour. As she never appeared to me 'full on' I often found this encounter frustrating. I was desperate to find out who this might be and I have spent many years doing extensive research on the Mains Hall and during that time have uncovered many interesting facts. I knew about the Hesketh family who were here in Tudor and Jacobean times and the Fitzherbert-Brockholes who lived here during the Georgian period. However, knowing a thing or two about history, I quickly realized that my lady was not in the right dress for any of these periods … it was a mystery.

A silent visitor

One night, comfortably asleep in my new room, I awoke with a start. I had a distinct feeling that someone or something was in the room. My eyes, still not quite used to the dim light, searched every corner of the room. Then I saw her. At last, what appeared to be a full apparition. She seemed unaware of me and yet focused as she moved silently from the doorway towards the bed. I felt sure that she would approach my side and, as this has never happened to me before, I was very scared. But she did not approach my side, instead she seemed intent on heading towards my husband's side. As she moved I watched her every step, for step she did, although she appeared to walk around the room in total silence, which would be difficult for any living soul to do as the floorboards creak terribly. As she reached my husband's side, I saw her in what appeared to be solid form. This in itself was quite unnerving and if you have seen a ghost yourself, you will perhaps agree that it can make you begin to doubt your sanity. I knew this was not a dream, however, as there is no mistaking the difference between a dream state and being awake. I tried to take in every bit of detail that I could. The bedroom curtains were open and the moonlight streamed into the room, allowing me to see her clearly. She wore the black three-quarter length velvet dress, with the white lacy detail about her neckline, and the same sleek hairstyle, parted neatly down the middle, and her skin was pale white. She did not look in my direction. She only gazed down upon my husband, who was oblivious to this dark stranger.

At this point I had to call out to my husband so that he, too, could see her. I took my eyes off her for a few seconds while I shook him awake, but when I looked back she had gone. My husband awoke but of course he saw nothing and had heard nothing.

After that one time, almost six months ago now, I have not seen her again in my room. I do still see her shadowy form in the usual places at the foot of the stairs, looking out of the window and also, oddly, facing a walled area near the stairs. And strangely enough, since that night, we often see a deep indentation on the bedclothes after having made the bed in the mornings, almost as if someone has been sitting there at the end of the bed. Objects have often been moved in this room, a hairbrush, a set of keys, my glasses to name but a few, only to 'reappear' elsewhere. Was she trying to draw my attention to her presence?

As time passed, all these things became the norm and we carried on with our daily lives with not a worry. Many psychics have visited the hall and I have been intrigued and astounded at how many of them can pick up on the fact that she seems to be here in the areas I talk about. Most tell the same story, that she is a lady who is looking out for her 'love'. She is deeply unhappy, because she feels he has deserted her. Some sensed the presence of a baby, too, and felt that she had perhaps lost a child, maybe in childbirth.

My story would have remained merely an interesting anecdote to tell friends, until another fateful event. As part of my research of the hall I had put a piece on a website inviting past residents or anyone who knew about the building's history to contact me. Imagine my surprise when a lady contacted me who had lived here and we had several conversations. She was amused to hear that we had so many ghostly 'others' residing with us, and as I began to describe in detail how 'my lady' appeared to me she became excited. 'The lady you describe so vividly sounds to me like the wife of a gentleman who used to lived there – she only ever wore black, she was very fashion conscious and wore her hair in the style of the day, slicked back and tied in a knot at the back of her head. She took great care of her appearance, wearing the pale make up of the day and bright red lipstick. She often wore a dress with a lacy collar, but she also favoured a double string of pearls too. She often spent her nights looking out of the window awaiting his return from "business".'

I discovered that it was her belief that this 'dark' lady was melancholic because she had lost a baby during childbirth. How odd then that my first nightmarish visions in that room had also featured a baby. Could this be 'my lady'? Did she die in this house, or was she merely a lost soul visiting a place she once lived? With this in mind I boldly offered up her name. 'Was her name Lily, by any chance?' I queried. The phone fell silent for some time. 'Hello…. are you still there? I can't believe what you are telling me', she gasped. 'It was my mother who was called Lily and she was not only the head housekeeper here, she was also a great friend and source of comfort to this lady of the house in times when she was most distraught.' It appeared the lady of the house had a troubled marriage. Her husband was cruel and neglectful. She became a sad and lonely figure, often spending hours gazing out of the window. In those days, a friendship with a servant would not have been acceptable.

These two women, however, had formed a bond and often the lady of the house called out when she wished to talk. 'Lily', she would call out towards the servants' quarters of the house, 'Lily....are you there?'

I had found out who 'my lady' was and the name I had heard or associated with her – Lily – was her friend and confidante. As we continued to renovate the hall we came across a hidden window behind years of plaster in the exact spot where 'my lady' stands often to this day, gazing longingly out towards the ancient riverbank in an attempt to see her husband return. I had apparently solved the mystery of my night-time guest. I still see her form in the same places on frequent occasions and still I greet her with the usual 'Good Morning Lily', though I think we both know that is not her name.

If you would like to take part in the on-going ghost investigations as Mains Hall visit the website at www.mainshall.co.uk

THE PSYCHIC MUSEUM

LOCATION: The Psychic Museum, York, England

DATE: 2002

TESTIMONY: Lionel Fanthorpe, Psychic Investigator

The astrologer Jonathan Cainer and a TV company with which he was collaborating, as part of the initial work in establishing the Psychic Museum at 35 Stonegate in York, had invited Uri Geller and me to check out the 600-year-old premises for them. I am not normally very sensitive to psychic phenomena, being a totally objective and open-minded scientific investigator in the Fortean tradition. All things are possible though. Nothing should be ridiculed or ruled out as impossible until it has been fully and fairly investigated, and this includes the workings of the human mind when psychic locations are being researched. That attitude goes with my Presidency of ASSAP (The Association for the Scientific Study of Anomalous Phenomena) and BUFORA (The British UFO Research Association). The most thoroughly proven and established facts should never be taken totally for granted. Even what seems to be the most apparently ludicrous nonsense should nevertheless be looked into seriously. Because of a characteristic lack of psychic sensitivity, I normally take one or two reliable and trusted mediums on investigations of this kind, but in the old house in Stonegate it was up to me on my own.

To my considerable surprise I did feel what I can only describe as an atmosphere. The house was old, and its ancient architecture suggested a psychic history. But what sort of psychic history? It was not a happy one. I did not see or hear anything in the way that sensitive psychic mediums report that they can, but I was aware of a presence – several presences – and the emotional waves (if that is what they were) that were radiating from them were unpleasantly negative. In a particularly active upstairs room, there were feelings of bitterness, jealousy and a desire for cruel, sadistic revenge. As I said, I saw nothing clearly and I heard nothing distinctly, but the impression was undeniable. The presence – if it was a presence and not just a replay from a 'stone-tapes' type of psychic recording – was of a woman in her late thirties or early forties. She might have been attractive in better circumstances or in happier times, but her face now gave an impression of acidic and twisted vengefulness. If 'hell hath no fury like a woman scorned', this desperately unhappy and furiously angry woman had felt scorned beyond endurance. Yet, underneath the anger and animosity in the psychic ethos of that room there were also twinges of guilt and remorse. If her dominant motivation had been vengeance, there was just a trace of conscience: the inescapable knowledge that what she was doing was wrong.

It was good to explore other rooms in the house that simply felt old without apparently containing any psychic traces, or harbouring anything that might have been interpreted as strange, sad, lingering, paranormal entities. What I thought of at the time as a cellar, but which would probably have better been described as a basement, was totally different from the neutral atmosphere of the majority of the rooms and the vicious, negative emanations of the sinister room upstairs. The cellar was full of fear. It was almost tangible – and it came from low down in one particular corner. Whoever, or whatever, was seemingly once terrified beyond bearing had been in that corner at some time in the past.

Who had once suffered in the cellar of 35 Stonegate? The victim in the Stonegate cellar seemed to be a teenage girl and her sufferings were apparently linked to the embittered, vengeful woman in the bedroom above. What could have gone so abysmally wrong in that historic house six centuries ago?

I stood in the cellar for a long time, looking into that fateful corner. Then I went back upstairs again, straining the last atom of my limited psychic sensitivity to establish a link between those two very different atmospheres. When I came back down into the cellar again, the vaguest outlines of a grim event from centuries ago were beginning to piece themselves together like a psychic jigsaw. The woman upstairs seemed to have been the mistress of the house when it had probably belonged to a prosperous, medieval merchant. She had been childless; or had borne children who had died in very early infancy. The poor little victim in the cellar seemed to have been a servant in that household, seduced by her employer – as so many young, female servants were – and consequently became pregnant. The childless wife's fury and jealous rage had subsequently been unleashed on the helpless girl. Chained in the corner of the cellar, she had been made to suffer. Her mistress's footsteps on the stone stairs had always heralded another savage beating – or worse.

Trapped on Earth

It is rarely possible to tell whether psychic sensations are the product of an honest – but fertile – imagination, or to distinguish between what is reaching it from the external world and what it is creating in response to its environment, or whether psychic energy exuded centuries ago is radiating from the fabric of an old building. It is never possible to rule out the chance – however remote – that actual, conscious, psychic entities that belong in another world are still trapped in ours, and somehow prolonging their sufferings here. As an ordained priest, and experienced exorcist, I suspected that the feelings I had at 35 Stonegate that day were so strong – both in the dismal cellar and in the bedroom above – that this was an occasion when someone might be trapped on Earth and needing spiritual help to move on. So I prayed for them both, whoever they might have been, prayed for their peace, forgiveness, reconciliation and future eternal happiness. As I did so there seemed to be a subtle change in the atmosphere, a lightening of the negative emotion, a reduction in the vengeful hatred and abject fear.

Right: The quirky roofs of the haunted museum reach for the skies, while strange and disturbing activities of a ghostly nature occur within.

Opposite: Lionel Fanthorpe, Psychic Investigator.

Then something else happened, something which was witnessed by the whole group. A porcelain doorknob appeared in the middle of the floor. It had not been thrown. It was no sleight of hand trick. I am experienced enough as an investigator to swear to that. The white, Victorian, porcelain doorknob simply appeared. It was a physically inexplicable apport. Was it connected in any way with the strange feelings that I had had concerning the bedroom and the cellar? Was that apported porcelain sphere meant to symbolize that a door had been opened somewhere and that something had passed through? All I know is that it happened, and that I can not explain it by any of our terrestrial laws of science..

Above: The Golden Fleece is one of York's most haunted hostelries, where the term 'rest in peace' takes on an all too sinister meaning...

HORROR HOTEL

LOCATION: The Golden Fleece Inn, Pavement, York, England

DATE: August 2002

TESTIMONY: Phylip De La Maziere, Psychic

In 2002 at the beginning of the autumn, I received an unexpected telephone call from a good friend inviting me to take part in a series of ghost investigations taking place in the city of York. Following a long drive from my home in Wrexham, North Wales, I was relieved to find that accommodation had been arranged for me at the Golden Fleece Inn, which was one of the places to be studied.

I was struck by the quaint old world charm of the inn as I entered and made my way into a dark, wood-panelled interior, with ancient beams that seemed to be just about holding up a plastered ceiling. After collecting my key I climbed the uneven staircase to the top of the building and Lady Peckett's Room, which was where I was staying. After changing and settling into my haunted accommodation I made my way back to the public areas to rendezvous with the rest of the psychic research team. It was now 7pm and the warm weather had been somewhat dampened by a sudden downpour, leaving an unpleasantly humid atmosphere. Would this be more conducive to ghostly activity, I wondered?

As the team assembled in the Lower Bar and enjoyed an excellent meal, I was gradually introduced to a variety of researchers who had travelled from far and wide in the hope of experiencing something unnatural at the inn. Little did I know that I was to be the one who would meet with the other side.

My work as a psychic has taken me to many places in search of the supernatural and, as we all swapped tales of this and that, our minds gradually attuned with the more sensitive subtle vibrations which permeate all time and space, and which would reveal themselves to me later that night. As the inn's usual customers slowly departed, leaving the psychic researchers to begin their work, I watched as the hands of an old clock edged their way towards midnight – the time traditionally associated with the spirit world. As the clock struck midnight we began planning our perambulations around the creaking building over the coming night.

No one had noticed the distinct drop in temperature as we had been sitting around an open fire until one of the inn staff commented on the peculiar chill which had crept into the bar. It was then that our first ghost was about to make itself known. Suddenly, the sound of the hand dryer in the gents' toilet was heard, yet no one had left the group and we were assured that no other living beings were

in the vicinity. The group hushed as we listened for anything further but the sound continued unabated. I decided to investigate and bravely strode up along the corridor to the doorway of the toilet. Followed by two ghost hunters, I slowly opened the door before walking boldly in and saw the dryer in full operation but no one in sight. Seconds later the dryer switched off leaving the small room in silence. To say a shiver went down my spine would be an understatement, but the best was yet to come.

We returned to the crackling fire in the bar and sat down quietly, wondering if anything else would happen. We had hardly recovered from our first encounter when a glass behind the bar flew off the shelf smashing loudly on the floor, making more than one of us jump out of our seats. Next a shadowy form was seen near the font door, which had been locked earlier by the staff. I decided to walk along the passageway to see if there was anyone playing a joke but was stopped dead by the manifestation of a man coming out of the wall dressed in Victorian clothing. He was clearly seen by me and two other members of the group as he walked across the passageway into the top bar before vanishing. Hearts thumping in our chests we were falling over each other to get back to the relative safety of the lower bar, and as we ran past the door to the gents' toilets the dryer was heard switching itself on once more. It certainly seemed that The Golden Fleece was 'alive' with the dead that night.

By now it was almost 2.30am and I was tired after my long drive and the night's activities, so I made my way up to bed. Not before I was warned by one of the ghost hunters that Lady Peckett's Room was the most haunted place in the inn. After closing the door and locking myself into the 'most haunted room' of the inn I took a quick shower and jumped between the crisp sheets for a well-earned rest and drifted off to sleep in no time at all. The next thing I recall is a loud 'bang' coming from somewhere in the pub which woke me with a start. I sat up in bed to look around the darkened room, the sound had seemed to come from nowhere. Moments later I was asleep once more, but I was soon to be disturbed again with the most frightening experience of my life.

A terrifying sensation

It began with the weird feeling of something like a cat walking up the bedclothes. I assumed I was imagining it and moved my legs around which seemed to make the sensation cease and for a minute all was still but then the feeling started again, so I moved my legs more vigorously and the feeling relented once more. By now I was wider awake and paying real attention to what was happening. I lay there in the dark waiting for the movements to begin again and my heart thumped in my chest so hard that I imagined I could hear it beating. Was it a cat that belonged to the pub perhaps? Or was it something else far darker and unimaginable? Could it have been the restless spirit of Lady Peckett herself for I had been told earlier that she often visits those that sleep in the room, or was it simply my own overtired mind playing tricks on me? What happened next left me in no doubt whatsoever that something from beyond the grave inhabits that bedroom.

Slowly raising my head off the pillow I strained my eyes to look around in the darkness, and there, standing next to the bed contained in a silvery ethereal light was a motionless figure. Its face contorted and deformed with a wry smile and exuding a sense of evil which came over me like a wave of dread. This thing was enjoying my fear, feeding off my terror. Its hollow eye sockets seemed to bore a hole into my very being and I was paralysed with abject horror as it moved closer towards the bed, its bony fingers touching the bedclothes and creating that all too familiar sensation I had endured minutes earlier. It came closer and closer, screams ringing in my head, unable to turn away or shut my eyes before suddenly in a flash of light it vanished, leaving me short of breath, drenched in sweat and an icy chill in the bedroom.

In a flash I was out of bed and grabbing a dressing gown I unlocked the door, my hands trembling to fit the key in the lock, before running down the stairs to the others in the bar two floors below. The rest of the night was spent in company downstairs and it was several hours before I could be persuaded to return to the bedroom to get dressed – this time accompanied by another member of the team.

After breakfast the next morning the organizer asked me if I had banged on his door during the night, 'No,' I replied, 'why do you ask?' 'Well there was one almighty bang on my bedroom door during the night, it sounded really angry.' Perhaps this was the bang I had heard resonating through the walls from the room just a short distance from my own.

At the time I did not know exactly who Lady Peckett was, but I know that she has a strong connection with the room which bears her name and in which I will never sleep again. I later discovered that the room is named after Lady Alice Peckett whose husband, John, owned the premises as well as being Lord Mayor of York around 1702. I know she is there for sure – I met her.

Above: Once a bustling mine, now it is just the shades of a haunted past that may be heard at The Cleveland Ironstone Mining Museum.

THE CHILDREN OF THE MINE

LOCATION: The Cleveland Ironstone Mining Museum, Teeside, England

DATE: October 2005

TESTIMONY: Mark & Angela Riley, Abbey Ghost Hunters

om Leonard had dreamt of opening a museum to preserve and display the history of the mining community for many years, but it was only when he met Tom Robinson, who owned the land upon which it now stands, that his dream came true. The museum opened in 1983, containing many items which had previously been displayed at Gisburgh Hall, but sadly Tom Leonard had died before its completion.

The discovery of the mine was first made in 1847 by Samuel Frederick Okey while he was walking on the beach at Skinningrove. He came across some ironstone nodules and investigated further. He later met Anthony Lax Maynard who told him there was an ironstone seam on his land. Okey sold the mine lease to Messrs Roseby, who commenced work on the 7 August 1848. The ironstone was hauled by horses to the base of the north and south drifts, and then to the surface by cable system. It was then weighed and tipped into railway wagons, before being shipped to Middlesbrough by rail. After temporarily closing in 1856, the mine reopened in 1865 before finally closing in September 1958. As you might expect, there had been many accidents over the years and several fatalities, including children. Inevitably, these gave rise to stories of ghosts and hauntings.

Staff who work at the museum today have often heard strange sounds, men's voices, drills drilling, horses and children playing – some staff have reported being touched by invisible hands. Abbey Ghost Hunters (a paranormal investigation team based in Scarborough) is run by husband-and-wife team Mark and Angela Riley and they were called in to help solve the mysterious happenings. They conducted two vigils to investigate the ghostly goings on which were disturbing the staff. They were accompanied on each occasion by their team.

Upon arrival we were taken on a tour around the museum by the staff. Angela, who is the team's psychic, sensed the spirit of a man called John who had once worked in the mine. She described that he would sit in the shop talking to visitors and was also very fond of pigeons. This was confirmed by a member of the staff who said that he used to sit in a chair in the shop telling anecdotes from his life as a miner to the museum visitors. One year after he passed away a pigeon flew into the shop and landed on 'John's chair', which could be taken as a sign that he was still around in some capacity.

The team were taken into an area named The Experience. It was in here that three investigators,

who all have psychic ability, said they could feel the presence of three children who were named Teddy, Jarvis and Ned. As this was being discussed one of the team members felt something breathe on her and Angela heard a small child calling out. As the staff watched on, one of them commented that he had heard his name called out by some anomalous voice in this area on many occasions, although no one had been around when he had tried to find out who was summoning him.

Table tilting and talking to Teddy

We decided to conduct a table-tilting session with some of the museum staff taking part. Almost immediately the table vibrated, indicating the presence of two separate spirits in the room. The entire team formed a circle of hands and tried to communicate with whatever might be with them in the room. We had set up a video camera to record what was happening, but this suddenly switched off.

The ten-strong team waited with baited breath as the séance began. The silence was broken after a short while by the sound of heavy footsteps, which were loud and deliberate and heard by every member of the team. It sounded as if they had come from above, yet 12ft of solid ground lay above the group. As an icy breeze whipped around our faces we decided to try our next experiment – direct spirit contact using a glass and the words 'yes' and 'no' written on pieces of paper placed on a table.

The museum staff made the first attempt at spirit communication. Standing in a circle, they each placed their fingers on the glass and asked aloud if any spirit were present. The sound of something heavy being dragged and a man's voice saying 'hello' assured us that we were not alone in the mine.

We moved to the Deputies' Room and made contact again, this time with Teddy, who psychic Angela said used to play in the mine and often watched the staff of the present-day museum. Teddy claimed that it was he who sometimes touched them and tugged upon their clothing. He said that other spirits also haunted the mine, including one which appeared as a frightening black shadow.

We moved into the Sound Room and heard a child's voice calling out 'get out'. At the time this was interesting but not acted upon. However, later on, when playing back some video footage which was taken of the area, you can see a black shape peering into the room, as if observing the team. Was this the voice of Teddy telling us to leave, knowing that the 'shadow' was in the vicinity?

I called out: 'Teddy can you make a knocking sound for us?' In response, two very loud bangs were heard echoing through the area. I then asked: 'Do you know what a Sprag is?' I knew that it was a type of mining tool. As we waited for an answer, the voice of a child shouted 'YES!' before fading away into the silence. Sadly young Teddy had become too tired to communicate further.

We decided to remain in the Deputies' Room to see if any other spirits would communicate with us, and we did not have to wait long until an angry man made himself known through Angela. He was not happy that the ghost team had brought women into the mine. They 'didn't belong in a man's place' he said. After verbalizing his disgust at the psychic he refused to communicate with her anymore and so we decided to try and talk to him through the glass and alphabet letters as we had done with the child spirit earlier.

Suddenly, the table thrust itself to one side. Angela said he was extremely angered by the involvement of the women. Again he thrust the table as if confirming what she had said. Next he showed his full force by shoving the table up to one of the ladies who was standing by, pinning her against the wall. Angela ceased the communication and left this upset and powerful man in the land of the dead where he belonged.

At the end of the night it had become clear that most of the spirits haunting the mine were benign. We had experienced audible and tactile phenomena and were sure that the mine was still haunted by echoes of its past.

Visit Abbey Ghost Hunters website at www.abbeyghosthunters.co.uk

Above: The Castle Keep has become a well known haunted location, and has stories of a variety of spectral residents.

THE SPECTRE INSPECTORS

LOCATION: The Castle Keep, Newcastle Upon Tyne, England

DATE: December 2005

TESTIMONY: Rachel Bell, Ghost-N-Spectres

Castle Keep sits high above the River Tyne on a site that has been the scene of nearly 2,000 years of turbulent and bloody history. It now stands at the heart of modern Newcastle, a monument to that city's prominent role in the history of the North East of England. The area has been occupied in one form or another since prehistoric times. Prior to the construction of the first castle buildings, the site was home to a Roman fort and then a Christian cemetery. The 'new' castle was first built as a motte and bailey structure in 1080 and then rebuilt in stone by Henry II between 1168 and 1178, in order to defend the county of Northumberland against the Scots. The Keep and the Black Gate nearby formed part of a much larger castle, of which only traces now remain.

Castle Keep was the scene of torture and death for many years and as part of the county's defensive network it had a garrison, and at one time was the county gaol. Many spirits are said to haunt the Keep. The most famous is the mysterious Poppy Girl, who is said to have suffered a horrific death while imprisoned at the castle. There have also been sightings of dark, hooded figures and of a gunner who lost his life in a tragic accident. Visitors have heard screams, unexplained noises and ghostly footsteps. Shadows have been seen moving around the gallery above the great hall and many visitors have captured mysterious images and light anomalies on their cameras.

The Ghost-N-Spectres team visited Castle Keep on 9 December 2005. The investigation commenced at 11.30pm, when those present were split into two groups and headed to separate areas of the Keep to keep vigil for ghosts.

A scent of flowers

The first group began in the King's Chamber by 'calling out' to any spirits present, and then attempted communication with a glass. The glass moved slightly, but there were no significant results which could be explained as paranormal. One thing that did occur was that a torch in an investigator's pocket was turned off suddenly. The group then had a short break before heading into the great hall. During the break, Simon, a lead investigator, took a small group into the mezzanine chamber, where they could detect a strong floral smell.

After the break most of the group took part in a Ouija board experiment in the great hall with the assistance of Ken, the medium, plus the warden at the Keep. The Ouija produced some interesting information, although nothing historically traceable was found. The group had apparently made contact with a small child and Ken said that he could sense that the child was sitting on the warden's knee. Meanwhile, some of the group had seen shadows moving along the gallery above the great hall and Simon led a group up to investigate. The gallery was found to be empty, but some of the group reported that they felt as though they were being watched. The group then headed down to the lower part of the Keep to continue the investigation.

The mezzanine chamber was chosen as the location for the beginning of the second part of the vigil. Here, several members of the group joined hands in a circle, while some members stood back to observe. While waiting in the darkness, a sound was heard on the stairs leading into the chamber and team members were able to see flashes of light with the naked eye that were also photographed. Believing that there was a spirit on the stairs, the team asked the presence to come and join them and a footstep-like noise was heard on the wooden floor next to them. A charged atmosphere was felt in the room and it seemed as though there was a ghost present which was responding to the requests for flashes of light to be shown. The garrison room was next on the list of vigil locations, here a further Ouija board session enabled the team to contact the spirit of a small child. Was this the same child that had been present earlier on in the night?

Left: Ghost Hunters frequently gather inside the Keep to try and decipher the secrets of the hauntings.

Meanwhile, the second group began their vigil in the chapel. I was part of this group and was the first to have a paranormal experience when I saw something pass by a window. Initially, I thought this was someone outside but upon investigation this was found to have been impossible as a scaffold had been erected there. The medium was next to sense something strange here, telling us that there were three different entities present, but that they were unaware of each other's presence in the chapel. As the medium was speaking, John, one of the investigators, shrieked when he saw a wisp of light moving across his camera lens. This is one of the most interesting light anomalies that Ghost N Spectres has ever caught.

In the garrison room we held a Ouija board experiment on the stone pillar. During the experiment, we contacted the ghost of a man who indicated that both he and his family had died inside the Keep. He told us he was a soldier and his wife and children were present with him in the spirit world. The Ouija board, rather amusingly, indicated that this man was very happy to be talking to the group, which consisted of only women. He considered himself to be a handsome man although not rich, and he indicated that his children would like a toy to be left in the chapel, so we left two of the toys we carry as trigger objects, but they did not appear to move during the rest of the evening. Later, I heard the sound of footsteps on a wooden floor which seemed to be following me across the museum area. At first I assumed this was a member of the team, but when I turned around there was no one there.

In conclusion, our investigation at Castle Keep produced some of the most varied phenomena the team has encountered. The flashing lights visible to the naked eye were perhaps the most exciting, and the lights were not only seen by those present but were caught on a night-vision camera, which is proof that they were not imagined by a heightened sense of anticipation. The wisp seen by group two in the chapel is also a particularly interesting occurrence. The group had checked the rooms prior to the investigation for any cobwebs or insects and no obvious explanation can be found for what was caught. In addition to this, auditory phenomena including footsteps were recorded, and the strong smell of flowers was also inexplicable.

Is Castle Keep haunted? Clearly further investigation is required, but many of the events of that evening have defied rational explanation and our investigation left the group eager to return to this fantastic location.

For information on Ghost-N-Spectres, and to watch the 'wisp' they caught on video at the Castle Keep, visit their website at www.ghost-n-spectres.co.uk

If you are brave enough to follow in the footsteps of Ghost N Spectres and visit the Castle Keep for yourself, information can be found here http://museums.ncl.ac.uk/keep/

Below: Illuminated by the flash of the camera, the interior of the Keep is clearly seen, but in the darkness who knows what may be lurking in the shadows?

TOUCHED BY THE DEAD

LOCATION: Dalston Hall Hotel, Carlisle, Cumbria, England

DATE: November 2004

TESTIMONY: Nicole Sheldon, UK Haunted

Dalston Hall is a fortified fifteenth-century manor house situated near Carlisle, Cumbria. History suggests that the area around Dalston Hall was first inhabited during Roman times. The Dalston family arrived with Robert de Vallibus, brother of Hubert de Vallibus, first Baron of Gisland, who was granted the land by Robert de Meschines, Earl of Cumberland, in 1301. Dalston Hall dates back to when the first John Dalston built a pele tower and dedicated it to his wife, Elizabeth, whom he married in 1507. At first, the tower stood alone.

The first floor consisted of the usual vaulted chamber (now the library) and later became a chapel, with the Ten Commandments painted on its walls. The spiral staircase was entered through an iron door. The two upper levels were a living room and a chamber. Above this was a fighting deck with battlements.

The family gained position in the counties of Cumberland and Westmorland. John's son, Thomas, increased the land possessions by purchasing from Henry VIII six manors and various monastic lands after the dissolution of the monasteries. As the family fortunes increased, Dalston Hall was enlarged, first with buildings on the east of the pele tower, then on the west. In 1664, the Civil War began and the Royalist commander, Sir Thomas Grenham, occupied Carlisle and was attacked by the Parliamentarian General Leslie, who used Dalston Hall as his headquarters. On 25 June 1665 Grenham surrendered and General Leslie took possession of Carlisle.

UK Haunted, a Paranormal Investigation Team, were invited to Dalston Hall in November 2004 to try and shed light on some of the ghostly goings on. Upon entering the building one could be forgiven for having the feeling of being taken back in time. The oak-panelled walls, adorned with paintings of people long gone, and soft candlelight, all added to the atmosphere of an era passed.

After a quick non-alcoholic drink in the bar, which is the area of most of the ghostly activity, the team began setting up the ghost-hunting equipment around the building. Cameras were strategically placed around the building, in those places where strange things had been reported in the past. After a brief walk around, the mediums, who had been asked to attend, reported that the cellar was incredibly active with paranormal sensations, so we decided to set up a trigger object. A wine bottle cork was placed on a shelf in the cellar; the door was then locked and nobody was allowed back inside unsupervised.

We were joined by members of the public from all over the country. As soon as everyone had arrived, we sat down at the dining table in the baronial hall, to a three-course meal. It did not take long for the conversation to turn to the spectral activity at Dalston Hall. Some people were apprehensive, others excited and a few very sceptical. Once the dining table had been cleared, everyone joined hands around it for a séance, which we hoped would begin to stir up the spirits, so to speak.

Bad-tempered Ian

At first, not much happened apart from one or two people feeling cold. Suddenly, one of the mediums, who is usually very quiet and reserved, began shouting profanities at everyone. It was obvious he was channelling the spirit of someone unpleasant. He gave his name as 'Ian', and asked everyone to leave 'his' house. One of the female mediums refused to leave, and 'Ian' began banging his fist on the table, frightening some of the ghost hunters.

Next one of the team suddenly complained of feeling as if he was on fire. No sooner had he spoke, than he collapsed and fell into the lap of a fellow researcher. The ghosts were certainly out that night. Two colleagues ran to his aid and carried him outside for some fresh air. Even though he was only of slight build, we had difficulty carrying him. It was as if he was much heavier than his usual weight. It was at this time that we decided that the séance should be brought to an end. We took a short break to calm down, and some of the ghost hunters, excited by what they had just witnessed, decided to wander around the building by themselves.

John, the medium who had channelled the spirit of Ian, decided to walk around the building to see what he could find. He was accompanied by several other researchers. As they were walking back down the main staircase, John cried out 'Watch out'. His warning came too late and one of the researchers fell down the last three stairs and landed on the hard wooden floor. Much to everyone's relief she was uninjured. She described the feeling of someone pushing hard at the back of her knees, deliberately trying to cause her to lose her balance. We all agreed it was now time to split into two smaller groups and explore as much of the building as the night would allow.

One group was keen to do a vigil in bedroom four. They heard the usual raps and creaks, but no concrete evidence of the paranormal. Some of the researchers began feeling sick and they were all terrified to enter the bathroom. The medium who was accompanying them described how he had 'seen' a young lady who, he claimed, had collapsed and drowned while taking a bath. Could this explain the group's fear and apprehension, or was mass hysteria to blame? Following the investigation, we could not find any evidence to substantiate the medium's claim. It could very well have happened, but there are no records that we could find of the event ever occurring.

The second group bravely decided to venture into the cellar. As soon as they descended into the murky gloom things began to happen which we could not explain. While holding hands and asking the

Below: The fire may warm those sentient visitors to the hall, but the cold chill of unseen spirits can still be experienced in the fifteenth-century manor house.

spirits of the cellar to make themselves known, the trigger object, the cork, flew off the shelf, and landed quite some distance away. This, it appeared, was evidence of the presence of a ghost. Nobody was anywhere near the cork when it launched into the air.

It was John, the medium, who first made psychic contact with an entity in the cellar. A non-human entity that exuded a feeling of pure evil. He earned the nickname of Mr Fingernails due to his long bony hands and claw-like nails which John described. As the vigil progressed, several people complained of feeling faint. It was then that John shrieked out in pain. He had felt something scratch his skin beneath his clothing. John lifted up his shirt to reveal three long fresh scratches, running from his chest to his navel. They were red and deep and had clearly been made by something sharp. No one present could have been responsible as we had all been holding hands during the cellar vigil, forming a protective circle.

The group decided to leave the cellar and Mr Fingernails behind and head for the relative safety of the bar. During coffee, we all exchanged experiences and the atmosphere was electric. By now, the mediums were all drained of energy and needed to rest. It was clear that the entity in the cellar was potentially dangerous and powerful but some researchers wanted to return to see if they would experience anything themselves. Six members of the team each took it in turn to venture into the cellar, but every one refused to step off the bottom step when they got to the bottom. The inky blackness filled them with dread. Several people said they had felt very sick as they descended the steps, which may have been explainable as fear mixed with anticipation but the presence of the entity might also explain the sensation.

At 4am the entire team met for the last time in the baronial hall for a debriefing and to draw conclusions from the night's events. Everyone present had experienced something they could not

explain in logical terms. The most interesting aspect of the debrief was the revelation that the entity Mr Fingernails, who had apparently attacked John in the cellar, had been experienced before. Apparently, a cleaner who was polishing in the baronial hall watched as a dark shapeless 'shadow' came up through the floor from the cellar and manifested in front of her, leaving her terrified and shaken. She did not recover for some time afterwards.

We concluded the investigation of Dalston Hall and retired to our respective bedrooms for some well-earned rest, but the ghosts had not yet finished with us – there was more to be experienced at Dalston.

Later in the night, in bedroom 19, one of the ghost hunters sensed the presence of a man in the room. This man was not happy about having his space invaded. After striking up a conversation with him, the ghost hunter, who is also a medium, pointed out that he was only there for a few hours sleep and would be leaving soon. This seemed to calm the angry spirit and for a few seconds a huge, bright orb danced around the mirror on the dressing table, before disappearing into the wall.

Meanwhile, footsteps were heard pacing slowly up and down the corridor outside the bedrooms. The strangest thing about this was that the footsteps sounded as if they were walking on a stone floor, yet a thick plush carpet had been laid in the corridor.

The ghost hunter, who was trying to sleep in bedroom 19, immediately ran into the corridor to see if anyone was playing a joke, but there was nobody around. Moments later nervous chatter came from the room 18. The researchers were packing their overnight bags and subsequently left in the middle of the night. It later transpired that the orb which had gone through the wall from bedroom 19 had been turning the bathroom doorknob and shaking the door violently. This was witnessed by the two researchers in the bedroom, and they did not stick around to see what else might happen.

Right: Although a good night's sleep cannot be guaranteed at Dalston Hall Hotel it is still the perfect retreat for a weary ghost hunter!

Over breakfast, the team discussed the unsettled night's sleep many of them had experienced. Two researchers, who spent the night in room four, reported that they observed a bible open itself to a particular page. They closed the book and settled down for some sleep, only to wake to find the bible opened up again at the same entry. In the same room, they witnessed a drawer open by itself, pulled by unseen hands. They had also left a hair dryer in the bedroom and were too afraid to return to collect it following breakfast.

At Dalston Hall you can expect good food, pleasant surroundings and comfortable rooms, but be warned, a good night's sleep is far from guaranteed.

For further information on Dalston Hall and its ghosts visit their website at www.dalston-hall-hotel.co.uk

Above: Disembodied footsteps and bumps in the night disturb sleepers inside Monkton Old Hall.

WALLED UP ALIVE

LOCATION: Monkton Old Hall, Pembrokeshire, Wales

DATE: March 2004

TESTIMONY: Veronica Charles, Spiritualist Medium

I was fortunate enough to be invited to spend a long weekend at an old hall in Wales in March 2004. As a spiritualist medium I am used to dealing with what others find hard to comprehend, but I had not expected any such experiences at Monkton Old Hall – my visit was supposed to be a holiday. The Hall is a fourteenth-century house which was associated with monastic life and is situated outside the fortified town of Pembroke. It was originally thought to have been the prior's lodging house, but more contemporary research suggests that it was probably a guesthouse or hospitium, accommodating visitors to a nearby Benedictine priory, which was founded in 1098. The building sits atop a much older crypt or 'undercroft', which runs the entire length of the house.

Some aspects of the area's history have been forgotten, but it is known that the priory itself passed to the crown in 1414, to the Duke of Gloucester, and subsequently it came into the possession of St Alban's Abbey in 1443. When the priory was dissolved in 1539 the Hall had several different owners before falling in status and becoming a simple farmhouse, which was subdivided and rented to minor gentry families in the eigtheenth century. In 1879 the Old Hall caught the attention of a wealthy lawyer named J. R. Cobb. He was a keen antiquarian and had the means to restore the now neglected building. Following extensive repair work, the building was returned to its former use as a rented home but sadly became uncared for once more over the decades until its second rescue in the 1930s. Miss Muriel Thompson, a journalist from London, had fallen in love with the place and following a long negotiation finally took possession in 1933. She devoted the remainder of her life to the house, ensuring its long-term future. When she passed away in 1978 she bequeathed her beloved home to her goddaughter Cheryl Campbell who subsequently sold it to the Landmark Trust in 1979. The trust's vision would continue Muriel's valuable work, and following some remedial repairs and structural alterations the Hall was made available for self-catering holiday-makers in 1982.

On the first night I slept in the small bedroom right at the top of the house, which is reached by a narrow, winding stone staircase and has pleasant views of the surrounding area. I was awoken in the dead of night by a finger knocking loudly and purposefully on a wooden surface, I assumed this must be a 'spirit' and as I was tired I ignored it and asked that it leave me in peace, which it did. The

Above: Vines creep around the garden arch, as the spirits of those long-gone creep around the Old Hall.

next morning I read in the guestbook that during the 1980s many people who had stayed in the house had reported hearing disembodied footsteps in my bedroom, and that the door had been known to bang shut of its own volition. Unworried by these minor spirit disturbances but intrigued by the haunting, I decided to carry out a small psychic investigation of the house. This was to be a busman's holiday after all.

After a day visiting local haunts I made my way up the stone staircase once more. I wondered what the night may have in store for me this time, and I was not to be disappointed. At 3.30am a strange sound echoed around the room. It reminded me of a whip crack or thunderbolt and seemed to reverberate around the stone walls, charging the atmosphere with that intangible something which indicates the presence of a ghost. I closed my eyes and my head was filled with the image of two women. The word 'sister' was ringing in my ears. I scrambled for a notebook in the dark to record my feelings before spending the rest of the night in a deep sleep – tomorrow night I would conduct my ghost hunt.

On the third evening a sombre atmosphere pervaded the Hall, like an aura of expectancy. Outside a bracing wind was howling and the sky was an ominous grey. I laughed at myself as I realized the situation sounded like it had come from the pages of Edgar Allan Poe. I lit a solitary white church candle and some incense and crept quietly down into the crypt beneath the house, hoping that the Hall would reveal some of its spectral secrets.

Sister Beatrice and the menacing monk

As I slipped into a psychic trance the first presence I contacted was a gentleman called Tom. He was a portly sort and looked as though he might have been a one-time gardener or workman. As I walked over to the fireplace and touched the rough stone the image of the two women who had visited me in the bedroom on the previous night returned, but this time more information was coming through. One of them was a woman with a deeply religious association. She told me she was a Carmelite nun named Beatrice. I felt that the other woman was connected strongly to Tom and to the bedroom at the top of the house in which I was sleeping. I understood now why I had heard 'sister' in my head on the previous night. I had hardly managed to assemble my thoughts when my vision was blurred by a different entity which stepped between us. A dark and malevolent force that manifested as a tall man swathed in black. His face was hidden from view beneath a large hood and an unsettling sense of menace exuded from him. I stood my ground and refused to be intimidated by this entity which now stood before me – its piercing eyes full of rage. Pictures filled my head of a woman abused by this vile man who hid behind the cloth of the church, a desperate suicide attempt and the sound of this man's boots echoing around the Hall. I decided to break contact and come back to the land of the living and as I came out of the trance the shadow of the phantom slid into the dark corner of the crypt like a receding enemy.

Back in the main house I set about collecting information about the Hall from various local books and pamphlets. I was not surprised to read that the spectre of a ghostly nun is reputed to walk at the Hall and in the grounds of the former priory and church. Sightings of this ghost are well attested and even the local vicar admits to seeing her and reports that she is most active around Easter time. Further entries in the Hall's guestbook detail other encounters previous holiday-makers have endured, such as loud footsteps, and whispering in the cross passage. But the account that caught my attention the most was an entry from which I quote: 'We were greeted by the ghost immediately upon arrival – three of us heard a woman saying "hello" and then friendly laughter.' I did some research about the Carmelite order and discovered that despite living an existence devoted only to God some nuns did branch out into the wider community to help others. Could Sister Beatrice be the phantom nun of Monkton Old Hall? The name Beatrice is of Latin origin and dates back to the fourth century and it was widely used in England throughout the middle ages.

Next I tried to find mention of a Tom and although his first name is not recorded there were several instances of a Mr James who was a gardener and workman employed by Miss Thompson, along with his wife who cooked and cleaned the main Hall from 1945 onwards. This was a possible connection between Tom and one of the ladies I had met in the Crypt. Was she his wife? Maybe they had shared a bedroom at the top of the staircase during their employment at the Hall which could explain the connection with that chamber.

This was all speculation and critics would rightly say that I have pieced together a story from unrelated facts, but it is not as easy to dismiss the malevolent presence which had interrupted my trance in the crypt. As I delved deeper into the Hall's history an old account about the nearby priory church pointed toward a possible identification of this unsavoury character. The document indicated that contemporary restoration of the church had unearthed an alarming find when the room above the porch, the Parvisse, was opened and the skeleton of a monk was found in such a position to suggest that he had been locked in alive. Another gruesome find was discovered when the floor of the knave was levelled and hundreds of human bones was found mingled in a most extraordinary fashion; skulls, legs, ribs and other remains lay side by side or crossing over each other without any order or arrangement of any kind. These were reverently collected and reinterred in a large communal grave in the shadow of the north wall of the churchyard.

So why was this monk walled up? What was his crime? Could he have been the dark force that had made itself known to me during my communication with Monkton's old haunts? Perhaps we shall never know the truth for sure. I left the house the following morning and have not returned since. I am sure that as long as the friendly spirit of Sister Beatrice, Tom and his wife remain at the house the force of the dark monk will be unable to cause trouble. Their presence will ensure that all is at peace at Monkton Old Hall – just as Miss Thompson would have wanted.

Monkton Old Hall is owned by The Landmark Trust and is available for holiday lets through their website at www.landmarktrust.org.uk

Above: The dank catacombs beneath Edinburgh still stir with activity; as the spirits of Mary King's Close go silently about their business...

GHOSTS OF THE FORGOTTEN LANE

LOCATION: Mary King's Close, Edinburgh, Scotland

DATE: February 2006

TESTIMONY: Ryan O'Neill, Scottish Paranormal

Mary King's Close is well known throughout the world. The history of this unique place is fascinating and working in this ancient site is like stepping back in time. I find it a great privilege to be able to conduct paranormal investigations here and am grateful to the staff of Mary King's Close and the Continuum Group for taking such an avid interest in the supernatural explorations we have undertaken.

Mary King's Close consists of a number of lanes which were originally narrow streets with houses on either side, reaching up to seven storeys high. In 1753, the Burgh Council decided to develop a new building on this site, the Royal Exchange, which is now the City Chambers. The houses at the top of the Close were knocked down and part of the lower sections were kept and used as the foundations for the Royal Exchange. The remnants of the lanes were left beneath the building; they are now dark and ancient dwellings steeped in mystery and intrigue.

For this investigation I decided which areas would be under surveillance well in advance. We split the location into three zones to ensure every area was effectively covered with constant environmental recording, visual recording and paranormal investigator witnesses. We began at 10pm and set up various trigger objects in Cheney's House, the Plague Room and Annie's Room, while also monitoring the back corridor connecting the Cattle Shed and Annie's Room. The Cattle Shed was covered visually by a night vision camcorder as was the Plague Room and the stairs leading down to the lower levels. In various areas we also placed data loggers which would effectively pick up any strange changes in the environment. We now had the equipment in place and it was time to get the investigation under way.

While one group conducted a séance with the aid of our highly skilled psychic medium in the Murder Scene area, a small team conducted a vigil in Room Four, which sits at the top of the Close. It was here that some of the best activity I have ever witnessed from a Scottish Paranormal investigation was about to take place.

It all started with the medium, Diane, sensing two small children in the area. I requested that we get a standard temperature reading along with an electromagnetic level recording. This is when the activity began. First there was a gradual drop in temperature in the vicinity. There was about a 6°C fluctuation which seemed to me an unusually high change. At this point two investigators, Graham and Lynsey,

reported a cold spot around them and this was certainly tying in with what was being recorded scientifically on the equipment in operation. Next some audible knockings and tappings were heard in the room. I have no natural explanation for these and it was startling that the combination of temperature change and sound phenomena occurred at the same time. The team experienced over 30 minutes of continual phenomena in the room, while Diane described various sensations as the spirits of children moved among us.

We asked the rest of the team, who had been researching a different area, to join us in Room Four to see if we could get more people to witness the paranormal activity. Ewan, who had previously not been in the room, described sensations which matched what Diane had been saying – even though he had not been party to her earlier findings. Other people, too, seemed to have the same kind of feelings associated with children. For me this was all extremely interesting as these team members had been separated at the start, and so cheating would be near impossible.

Unexplained energy

We moved into the Plague Room, where I instructed Dougie (one of the investigators) to take EMF readings. In the meantime the psychics took a few minutes to attune themselves psychically with this new area. In situations such as this I like the surrounding environment constantly monitored for any slight change that could signal an unexplained anomaly. It was not long before Dougie started to pick up a strong fluctuating magnetic energy field around Fiona. I monitored this very closely and was intrigued by the occurrence. It was not until Dougie started recording at a higher level above Fiona's head that I noticed an electricity cable that runs along the roof. The EMF meter was therefore displaying readings with a natural cause.

What was not in doubt in this area was yet another temperature drop recorded by investigator Dave between the Plague Room and the Cattle Shed. This was a gradual decrease and it seemed as unexplainable as the earlier temperature drop in Room Four. I am not sure what caused the drop in the temperature, but it adds to the various other unexplained phenomena witnessed in the Close that night.

As a paranormal investigator I look at a wide range of circumstances while on location and I try to explain them by firstly exhausting all natural causes. There are occasions when I cannot do this, and it has me thinking for weeks and sometimes months after the investigation. I have such a problem with what happened next, inside Chesney's House.

Investigators Rachel, Mary and Fiona went down into Chesney's House for a vigil before we finished. What was about to happen was completely unexpected. Earlier we had set up a trigger object and a video camera inside the house, along with a movement sensor which would sound an alarm if anyone entered the vicinity. As the team made their way towards Chesney's House they could hear what they described as a car alarm. They were in fact hearing the movement sensor which had been triggered by

something moving through the area. We played back the video tape which had been recording what was happening in the house and on the tape we saw that no one had crossed the sensor beam – at least no one we could see. Furthermore, the alarm can be seen stopping for a few seconds before continuing ringing throughout the Close. There is no natural explanation for this mystery.

Mary King's Close is a location I love to work in, I have been back time after time and something paranormal always happens. As a paranormal investigator it is a delight to investigate and always a hit with the tourists. Indeed, they now hold a GhostFest every year, celebrating its haunted history.

You can learn more about the investigations conducted by Scottish Paranormal on their website at www.scottish-paranormal.co.uk

Information on Mary King's Close, including opening times, ticket prices and 'GhostFest' can be found at www.realmarykingsclose.com

Below: It is easy to lose yourself in the labyrinth of passageways at Mary King's Close; but be warned - spirits abound around every corner...

Above: Castle Cary is being restored to its former glory by the current owner who lives at the castle with his family; and their ghosts.

A FACE IN THE WINDOW

LOCATION: Castle Cary, Bonnybridge, Falkirk, Scotland

DATE: April 2006

TESTIMONY: Stephen Lambert, Charity Ghost Hunts

Castle Cary is in Bonnybridge, a few miles north of Cumbernauld. Arriving by car can be quite tricky if you do not keep your eyes open, because the castle is hidden behind trees a little way off the beaten track. After a tour with the owner it was clear to see why the tower was built here. Big banks on three sides of the tower known as the Red Burn would have made it a hard place to attack. The Castle was built in 1478 and is in two halves. The original tower did have a wing, but all that remains of this are a few stones sticking out from the tower. Another wing was built in 1679.

Prior to my visit in April 2006 I had tried to keep my research to a minimum. Knowing as little as possible about the ghost stories at the castle had to be a good thing. I was aware, though, of a General William Baillie of Letham and an Elizabeth known as the White Lady, who was the daughter of a laird. These two people were supposed to haunt the castle and this was all I knew. I was also aware that Mary Queen of Scots had visited the castle in 1561. I think I was more worried about her than others. Not sure she would be happy with an English ghost hunter.

After speaking to Andrew, the present owner, over tea he explained how he had not seen any of the supposed ghosts, but had recently felt some cold spots. The only room he did not feel totally comfortable in was the old tower when alone. This was slightly strange because on my tour I had asked Andrew if the room was always as cold as it was. I felt myself a bit uneasy in the same room but had not heard his feelings at this point. During tea, I kept feeling cold spots on my arm. Doors were closed to discount drafts but still the cold feelings on my arms and legs kept coming and going.

At about 1am I found myself alone in the hall of the castle, which is now the living room of the present owners. This was my first time spent totally alone in a supposedly haunted location. Surprisingly, I felt very at home sitting with the night-vision camera on alone in the dark with no back up on hand via the walkie-talkie. Before long I was asking for spirits to come through. A couple of times there were some knocks in response to my questions. I feared all along for some reason that Mary Queen of Scots was going to appear in a wrathful state.

All was seemingly ok until about 2 to 2.30am when I heard some sort of crying or singing from upstairs. This lasted on and off for about five minutes. While taking pictures at this time I caught my

one and only orb in the doorway in the hall. I had taken pictures all day and had not picked up any orbs. So this in my mind discounted the dust theory.

That was about it for the night. The next morning when Andrew came down I explained what I had heard. Andrew himself had not heard crying or singing that night or in the past. He then went on to explain the story behind Elizabeth, the White Lady. In her father's eyes Elizabeth had been destined for a great marriage. She fell in love though with a laird from Lennox whose surname was Graham. These were the same Grahams who set fire to the tower during the years of the persecution. Her father was angry and ended up locking Elizabeth in the uppermost tower, feeding her on only bread and water. After hearing this I am sure that the crying had to be that of Elizabeth. She surely would not have been singing though.

The only possible sighting of General William Baillie of Letham was a photograph I took from the outside standing at the window that, I subsequently discovered, he always looks through. There is a small image in the middle pane of the second row down which looks like it could be his face.

Stephen operates Charity Ghost Hunts, *which arranges ghost hunts to raise money for charity. Visit his website www.charityghosthunts.co.uk for more information.*

Above: There appears to be a face looking out of this window at the photographer; ghost hunter Stephen Lambert. The same window, from the inside, is shown below.

Above: The Clock Tower at Pittenweem was once used as a holding place for those accused of witchcraft, now their ghosts linger here.

TERROR TOWER

LOCATION: The Clock Tower, Pittenween, Fife, Scotland

TIME: Spring 2005

TESTIMONY: Ryan O'Neill, Scottish Paranormal

Pittenweem is a beautiful little Scottish fishing village in the east of Fife, situated a few miles from Anstruther. By the turn of the eighteenth century prosecutions for witchcraft were becoming rare in Scotland, but not in Pittenweem. The clock tower is where those accused were tortured and imprisoned, including both men and women. We arrived at 7.40pm and met up with Lenny Low, the key holder, and James, a local reporter from the East Fife Mail. After introductions we made our way inside the haunted building which dates back to 1620. We began by setting up a low-light video camera to record the spiral staircase. In this way we ensured that if anyone entered the tower, they would be recorded visually on the tape. I instructed one of the investigators to conduct a series of baseline tests. These record the natural temperature, electro-magnetic energy and humidity within the alleged haunted site.

The tower is an impressive building and Len lost no time in conducting a short tour to introduce us to all the points of interest. Suddenly, the tour was interrupted by an almighty crash which came from the lower levels. We quickly descended the stairs, assuming our equipment must have fallen over, but nothing could be seen and we were unable to find anything to explain the source of the sound.

Feeling brave, we decided it was a good time to enter the dungeon. As we stood in the gloomy, dank darkness Len described the history of the surrounding village of Pittenweem. Today, the dungeon is used by the council as a storage space, but something of its terrible past still lingers in the atmosphere. After a short visit to a nearby cave we decided that the night vigils should begin. We set about dividing the team into small groups so that we could cover as much of the building as possible.

As we were deciding who should go where, the first paranormal manifestation took place. This was in the form of an intense temperature drop, which registered on our thermometer as 5° C down to over -2°. A rapid drop of over seven degrees which did not make sense as the ambient room temperature felt the same. One of the investigators, Fiona, walked over and stood directly in the centre of the area where the temperature had fallen and soon became aware of a spirit presence around her which seemed to be communicating through thought transference. The cold spot then shifted and as Fiona pointed to its new location and moved accordingly, we confirmed what she was experiencing by recording the movement on the thermometer.

Fiona described a female spirit who had suffered in the building many years ago. She was named Belle and had been accused of witchcraft. She found the accusation laughable as it was untrue and she said she was with others inside the tower who were in similar circumstances. The communication was fleeting and yet it had produced some specific detail which I could check out later.

When I found Len I wasted no time in asking him about the name Belle. He looked astonished and confirmed that a woman named Isabelle had indeed been accused of sorcery and tortured inside the tower. Furthermore, it took place in the very room in which Fiona had made the contact with her ghost. The information had not been released and was in his private archives and so there was no way Fiona could have had prior knowledge.

With the success already achieved by Fiona, Rachel was next to make contact with the presence of the past inside the tower. The name Robert was ringing in her mind and she asked Len if this made any sense. He answered that it was a name which had popped up in the records of the building many times. So we had another psychic hit and another ghost to add to the list.

After visiting other areas and rooms in the tower, without making further contact, we decided to wrap up the investigation, but not before Fiona made contact with a woman again. This woman was crouching with her legs huddled up to her body and had long black dirty hair. Was this a vision of Isabelle? Or was this another of the witches of the Clock Tower at Pittenweem?

You can learn more about the investigations conducted by Scottish Paranormal, including the Clock Tower, on their website at www.scottish-paranormal.co.uk

Above: At the centre of an ancient forest lies the gothic masterpiece Charleville Forest Castle.

HIDDEN HAUNTS

LOCATION: Charleville Forest Castle, County Offaly, Ireland

DATE: March 2002

TESTIMONY: Jason Karl, International Ghost Hunter, President of Ghost Research Foundation

Almost in the dead centre of the Emerald Isle, amidst a dark and ancient forest, stands the gothic masterpiece of architect Francis Johnston – Charleville Forest Castle. Perhaps the finest Gothic Revival castle in the whole of Ireland, this eccentric castellated mismatch of towers and buttresses was constructed over a fourteen year period commencing in 1798. In 1963 the castle became uninhabited for the first time in its history. The roof collapsed and the decay of the structure, which up until then had been kept at bay, increased in earnest. The castle's saviour came in the form of Michael McMullen who, deplored at its state, instigated restoration work in 1971, he was later succeeded by Constance Heavey-Seaquist and her daughter Bridget Vance, the latter continuing her restoration work to the present day.

I was to spend the weekend at the castle in March 2002, and with a bulging file of notes beneath my arm I found myself approaching the castle as the daylight dwindled late one blustery Friday afternoon. I had read of the alleged mass incarceration of those suffering from the black plague, entombed beneath the castle in an attempt to prevent the disease spreading. Stories of whispers in deserted rooms and sightings of the strange people glimpsed in the candlelight that illuminate the hallways (much of the castle is not yet connected to electricity) were also prevalent, and with a plethora of other activity from the spirit realm, blamed partly on the confluence of two ley lines beneath the structure.

I was due to meet the owner Bridget Vance and after walking up to the grand entrance and knocking on the front door I waited for it to be answered. After what seemed like an age, and with no reply, I pushed the creaking door open and stepped inside. It was then that 'the feeling' gripped me – an intense yet inexplicable sense of 'something' which is commonplace in the quiet, haunted, places of our world. The atmosphere was pierced by the sound of 'Hi!' from Bridget, who had emerged from a doorway beneath a Gothic balcony, sending the shadows fleeing into the dark recesses of the Entrance Hall.

After a warm welcome and some refreshment, I was invited to explore the castle by myself. Armed only with a torch for comfort and with a camera over my shoulder I climbed the wooden staircase and came to the end of the dais where Bridget had told me I would find a hidden portal; sure enough the warped panelling swung open to reveal a cobweb-filled stairwell. At the far end of the hallway I found

Above: After passing through the castle gates one finds oneself in a bizarre world where fact and fantasy meet.

myself in an octagonal library. I had read about this room – the former inner sanctum of the brotherhood of Freemasons, ordered by a former Earl who was a Grandmaster of the sect. I was standing in the eight wall construction in which their secret rituals had once been conducted. Who knows what arcane rites these walls had observed, and if they could talk – would they dare tell? Not wanting to linger, and keen to make a whistle-stop tour of the main areas whilst the light remained, I began looking for an exit. It came, after several minutes of examination, in the form of a secret sliding door at the back of one of the elaborately carved book shelves. Beyond, a glimpse of natural light spurred me on and I stepped from the library into a catacomb-like passageway, practically derelict and clearly open to the elements.

It was then that I heard the faint sound of distant keys being played upon a piano. The music seemed far away as from some chamber in a distant part of the castle. Retracing my steps, for the light was now fading fast; I quizzed Bridget as to the piano player. It was Katy – Bridget's daughter – who answered first, telling me that the sound of a phantom pianist had been reported before, and that although there were two pianos in the castle, one was in pieces and the other was un-tuned and in the dining room, and no-one had touched either for many months. I decided to try and replicate the sound by asking Katy to play some chords whilst I returned to the, now dark, catacomb passageway, to see if I could hear any trace of the sound. Unsurprisingly the experiment showed unequivocally that the tune I had heard was not made by the piano in the dining room. Perhaps it was an echo from a time long past, a momentary lapse into the shadow realm of Charleville's haunted past?

I wondered if Katy was perhaps susceptible to the sensitive psychic wonders within the castle; and indeed that seemed to be the case as she related stories of window shutters closing by themselves in her bedchamber, being locked in the nursery by an unseen key holder, and hearing the melancholy sound of a child crying in distant rooms. At other times footsteps could be heard in deserted hallways and the sound of heavy furniture being dragged had been heard by her aunt. Katy also told me that toilets flush of their own volition and taps are turned full on by invisible hands; once this resulted in a serious flood.

No need for a screwdriver...

The following afternoon I returned to the castle. My first task was to set up the library for a séance which I planned to hold at midnight. Bridget and her daughter Katy had agreed to join me and I was hoping that we might make contact with some of the building's long-gone inhabitants. In order to set up the library for the séance it was necessary to remove a large drawing board. It became obvious that I would have to undo the screws which were bolting the equipment together in order to get it through the small doorway, but I soon realised that a spanner was required and so set off to find Dudley – Bridget's partner, to ask if he had one I could borrow. A few minutes later I returned to the library only to find that the screws had been undone! Amazed, I asked Dudley if he had undone them for me. He insisted that only he, Bridget and I were inside the castle, and that neither of them had ventured anywhere near the library.

Bridget then told me that the spirits of the castle were friendly and this was a typical gesture of welcome to a famous ghost hunter!

As the night drew closer the wind was beginning to whip around the towers. I followed Bridget into the great 120 foot long gallery where she opened a cabinet and withdrew a small leather-bound book. We sat down before a roaring log fire and Bridget began to tell me the story of Harriet Hugh-Adelaide, perhaps the Castle's most frequent ghostly visitor. The third daughter of the third Earl of Charleville, Harriet Hugh-Adelaide was eight years old when she met a terrible fate at the castle. It was 3 April 1861 when she decided to slide down the banister of the twisting staircase; a playful act that resulted in a 20 foot fall to a tragic death. Since that day her ghost has been seen frequently about the castle. In 1993 Bridget's son Michael, who was four years old at the time, was discovered standing at the bottom of the staircase staring blankly up toward the top. Bridget was bemused when he spoke the words 'don't worry mummy, a little girl held my hand'. On another occasion, Katy, aged six at the time, announced 'I am going to my room to play with the little girl'; yet there was no 'little girl' in the castle at the time; and she was not the sort of child to make fanciful stories up. Sheila Stewart, Dudley's daughter, and two of her friends had an encounter with Harriet in 1998. As they walked towards the stairwell they were surprised to see a young girl walk out of the door in front of them, dressed in a white dress and blue apron. No sooner had they seen her than she turned and walked back through the door. Upon examination no trace of her ever having been there could be found.

Charles or Connie?

It was now time to make our way to the library for the séance. I had placed a mirror and candle upon the mantelpiece in the hope that the light might coax the spirits from the beyond using the ancient glass as a gateway between their world and ours, and as we sat in the flickering candlelight I began to speak to the spirits of the beyond. 'Give us a sign', I asked, 'Come through to us now, lift the veil, let your presence be known to us', I continued, eyes tightly shut in the hope that something of the supernatural might grace us with their divine, undead, presence. After a few moments I felt the icy touch of something on my left ear. Gentle but distinct, a definite brush with something which was here, and yet could not be seen. Bridget began laughing madly, 'it's the ghost of Charles!' she said, 'he thinks you're cute'. Both alarmed and amused by her comment my expression demanded further explanation and so she told me that a former Earl – Charles William Bury the second, despite having a wife with whom he lived at Charleville, had enjoyed a series of intimate liaisons with Lord Byron who had visited the castle during the early 19th century.

As the energies were building it seemed the perfect time to ring the bell – a beacon of sound which it is believed can be heard both on the physical and the astral planes, a kind of magnet to which the spirit of Charles might come closer to us. I rang the bell at the north, south, east and west quarters of the table and after sitting down again the light dimmed. The flame of the candle illuminating the antique mirror was depleted, almost horizontal – as if a strong inexplicable breeze was blowing out from behind the very glass itself. 'If you are the spirit of Charles Bury the second, give us a sign', I asked. In immediate answer I felt again the icy touch of a bony finger, this time across the back of my head – stroking my hair. By now the room had become intensely chilled and the sense of a brooding presence was very strong. We decided that we had come close enough to Charles and bade him farewell, telling him to return to the realm of shadow and to leave us in peace. After the room had warmed and the candlelight had settled, it was Bridget who first spoke. 'My mother Connie was here too' she said, 'I could feel her presence with us; she would have loved a séance!' As we extinguished the candles and made our way back to the relative safety of the gallery I wondered if we really had encountered the ghost of the spirited Earl, or whether it had been Bridget's mother indulging our supernatural curiosity? Either way, I was satisfied that we had made contact with the other side.

The rest of the night passed quietly, and the next morning I descended the grand staircase and made for the front door, closing it firmly behind me and pausing as its echo rung through the many empty chambers of the castle. It was St Patrick's Day, and as Ireland celebrated I hoped that the ghosts of Charleville Forest Castle might be doing so too. My weekend of gothic horror was now over, but I would be haunted by its memory for years to come.

Above: The spirit of a lady was caught on video looking out of the window of a holiday home in France in November 2001.

THE HAUNTED GITE

LOCATION: Vendée, France

DATE: November 2001

TESTIMONY: Jane Powers, Witness

While visiting France in November 2001 with my cousin Ken, and his wife Angela, we stayed with his brother who now lives in France permanently. We stayed in a 200-year-old gîte on his property, and which he lets out to holiday-makers during the summer months. It was on the last evening of our stay that Angela and I were talking in one of the rooms on the first floor when she suddenly shivered and said: 'Someone just walked behind me!' Despite being a little spooked by the experience we laughed it off and slept peacefully.

The next day Ken was locking up the gîte before we went out for the day. He pulled the shutters across the inside door and the lever, which is usually hard to move, moved up and down of its own volition. Being a down-to-earth kind of man this did not bother him and he made light of it as we left for the day.

Later that day we returned to my cousin's house before travelling to the airport and I thought it would be nice to record some video footage of the gardens and gîte to show my family once I had returned to England. The gîte was still locked up and no one had been inside since we had left earlier in the morning. The rest of the party had gone back to the main house and I was left alone to wander around with my video camera. I began by walking towards the gîte, happy that I was able to take some fabulous shots of the outside, even though the inside was inaccessible. I then walked through the gardens to take some further footage.

Upon returning home and viewing the video images my husband, who had been unable to accompany me to France, was first to notice an 'extra' on the tape. He came into the kitchen and asked me who had been inside the gîte while I was taking the video. I answered that no one had been inside. He said: 'There is someone in there passing by the window.' We hurriedly rewound the tape and there sure enough was a figure moving past the windows as I was walking up to the ancient building taking the video.

Several members of the family have seen the video and could not determine what exactly was on the tape, so I sent it to some psychic researchers who were equally unable to explain it. When you watch the images in slow motion you can clearly see a figure, which appears to be looking out of the window and moving out of the way of the camera.

I later discussed the video tape with Angela and we talked in more depth about the presence she had felt walk behind her in the gîte. Upon reflection she had not felt in any way threatened. I speculated

whether it was the ghost of the old lady that had moved out of my cousin's house a year earlier. She had killed herself by jumping off a bridge into the river way below. But Angela said 'no, although it was definitely a lady, I think she died by hanging.' I pushed her for more information but she would not comment further and could not explain why she felt anything at all. She is not usually psychic and does not profess to have special abilities.

I returned to the gardens of the gîte with Angela a little while later to see if we could feel anything for a second time, but there were other guests staying and as we did not want to disturb the ghost and perhaps spoil their holiday we decided to leave her in peace. I did discover that the gîte was originally a bakery, could this help explain the ghost lady in the video? She does appear to be wearing a white 'leg of mutton' type sleeved blouse – could this be the dress of a baker?

The names of the witnesses in this testimony have been changed to protect their identities.

THE MONK OF CARCASSONNE

LOCATION: Carcassonne, Languedoc-Roussillon, France

DATE: Summer 2005

TESTIMONY: Phylip De La Maziere, Psychic

This is not a ghost story that features frightening apparitions, headless horseman or phantom hounds, neither is it about things that go bump in the night. Instead, it is a true tale of events which happened to me and my wife, Jean, in the early summer of 2005 when the Cathars, the Freemasons and the medieval city of Carcassonne came together for a brief moment.

The walled city of Carcassonne, in the southwest of France, stands on a plateau dominating the landscape for miles around and overshadows the modern city. The thick stone walls have managed to withstand the incursion of much of the modernist architecture in this otherwise beautiful city.

It was here during the thirteenth century that a bloody crusade was directed by the Roman Catholic Church to crush and destroy the heretical sect of Cathars. This 'Cathar Castle' was the setting for our well-earned break in 2005. My ancestors have connections with either the Knights Templar or the Cathars and I wanted to walk in their footsteps.

It was midday when we first caught sight of Carcassonne. The sun was blazing in a perfect blue sky and the dust hung above the road as cars sped towards the château city. A short walk through the magnificent stone gatehouse and we were inside. All around us were towers and ramparts – we really had stepped back in time. Already I was feeling a sense of harmony with the place. The hundreds of tourists bustling around did nothing to distract me from the more subtle emanations from the narrow streets and overhanging buildings. The feeling of the past was strong here and readily accessible to anyone who would take the time to pause and look around.

After making our way, simply following 'where the spirit would take us' rather than a map, into a fine cobbled courtyard we found ourselves in front of the ruins of an old abbey. Taking the opportunity to rest in the afternoon shade we noticed, not far away, a church where tourists were congregating. It was while observing this scene that both Jean and myself became aware of a soft chanting. Jean said: 'The acoustics are strange here, I can't quite make out from which direction the sound is coming from. It must be a choir.' The sound was clearly a chorus of voices, presumably coming from within the church. It was so beautiful and haunting that we wanted to investigate further, and so we made our way inside the church, expecting to find the source of the chanting which by now had stopped, carried away on the

breeze. But there was no choir, no priests and no explanation for what we had heard. Just the usual array of camera-snapping tourists with sunburnt faces and ice creams. Somewhat puzzled we left the church, then I noticed a small alleyway off the beaten track and glimpsed a sign for a bookshop. I wondered if they might have anything in English and we made our way into the shadow of the alleyway.

An icy surprise

To my surprise and delight the bookshop owner, Raymond, had a fine grasp of English. I was soon engrossed in conversation with him about the city, telling him of my ancestry and the reason for our visit. Glancing down I noticed that he was wearing a Masonic ring (black onyx set with a gold square and compass). Raymond noticed my interest and asked if I was a Freemason. He offered me his hand which I shook in a certain way, to indicate that I was part of the brotherhood. Realizing my obvious interest he told me of a Masonic Lodge within the city walls called Lodge St Jeanne d'Arc (Lodge of Saint Joan of Arc). He asked if we might like to see it and within minutes the bookshop was locked up and we were following Raymond, at great pace, through the labyrinth of backstreets of old Carcassonne.

When we arrived at the ancient wooden doors which seemed to stand taller than the city gatehouse itself, Raymond lost no time in ushering us inside before closing the doors from prying eyes. We were in a long corridor with doors leading off on either side. This was where the brothers would don their ritual robes before entering the Lodge itself. We followed Raymond down the corridor and he let us into the central chamber. As the light illuminated the grand room, Jean noticed a monk standing in a doorway observing our visit. 'We are being watched', she said, nudging my arm and indicating the doorway. 'Oh, he's gone!' she exclaimed, 'he was there a few seconds ago.' I decided to follow the figure as I was keen to meet another Brother of the Lodge, but as I began to descend the staircase in the doorway I met with an icy chill which penetrated my body. 'Crikey', I shouted, as I stumbled forward, trying to catch my breath which had been whipped from my lungs by the intense temperature change. The feeling of intense oppression, sadness and decay was overwhelming and as I regained my composure I saw the figure standing at the bottom of the staircase, staring at me. I said 'Bonjour', but he just smiled at me before turning and disappearing through another doorway. I climbed back up the staircase and returned to Jean in the great chamber. 'Did you see him?' Jean asked. 'Yes, for a moment', I replied, before making my way out of the Lodge and down the corridor to the front doors, Jean following behind.

Mystified by our encounter with the monk in a pale blue habit we retraced our steps and found our way back to the bookshop. Raymond had prepared three cups of tea and was awaiting our return. 'Did you enjoy your visit to the Lodge?' he asked. We replied that we certainly had. After a few minutes Jean asked: 'Why is there a monk in the Freemason's Lodge, is he looking after the building?' Raymond almost choked on his drink, wide-eyed and clearly frightened he looked at us quizzically and asked: 'By chance has anything else happened to you today, regarding monks?' 'Only the chanting we heard

earlier near the abbey ruins', I said. Raymond had a smile upon his face. 'There are no monks in Carcassonne anymore. They haven't been here since the Crusade when the Cathar monks, rather than denounce their beliefs, threw themselves off the tower which is now part of the Lodge building.' He went on to tell us that the sound of plain-chant had been heard in the city before and that many Brothers had seen a sad-faced monk standing watching the Masonic ceremonies in the Lodge. Interestingly, it has only recently been discovered that the Cathar monks did wear habits of pale blue material, just as we had seen in our glimpse into the past.

Being a psychic I am not surprised that we had somehow connected with the spirit of Carcassonne, my ancestry and membership of the Brotherhood may have all compounded the supernatural experience we had in the medieval city that summer day. It is a day I will never forget and I hope to visit it again soon – to meet once more with the friendly spirit of the monk of Carcassonne.

If you fancy hunting for the ghostly monks of Carcassonne, information on accommodation and opening times can be found on the city's website at www.carcassonneinfo.com

Above: Sensations of a sinister past were felt during a visit by psychic investigator Lionel Fanthorpe to Wewelsburg Castle in Germany.

TORMENTED SOULS

LOCATION: Wewelsburg Castle, Büren, Westphalia, Germany

DATE: 2000

TESTIMONY: Lionel Fanthorpe, Psychic Investigator

While I was presenting the Castles TV series for the Discovery Channel, we were working in the torture dungeons at Wewelsburg Castle in Westphalia, Germany. Notorious during the Nazi era as the headquarters of Heinrich Himmler's SS, Wewelsburg Castle stood over a Neanderthal burial ground, a Bronze Age settlement and a Saxon stronghold. If ever a site was vulnerable to whatever strange, psychic influences may permeate the fabric of the Earth and ancient structures, it was Wewelsburg. Germany's bloody-minded seventeenth-century Episcopalian princes – who seemed obsessed by the concept that pain and death were essential ingredients of religion – had attacked any vestige of supposed witchcraft with single-minded fanaticism.

It is not possible to estimate how many innocent women and girls screamed out their agonized 'confessions' in those dungeons, and were then executed for witchcraft, heresy – or both. Something of their indescribable suffering seemed to be lingering in Wewelsburg centuries after the wind had blown their ashes from the stakes where they had died. Even a solid, pragmatic investigator with as little psychic sensitivity as I have got could feel it distinctly. Our equally tough, professional film and sound crew discussed it while we worked, and we all more or less agreed that whatever was responsible for the strange Wewelsburg atmosphere, the sooner we could finish the job and get out – the better.

Having finished filming in the cellars, we went up to the room that Himmler's SS had used as a ceremonial centre for whatever kind of sick, evil ritual had passed for religion among them during their days of power. The atmosphere up there was – if possible – even worse than the atmosphere in the torture dungeons below. In those subterranean hell-holes, sadists had tortured the innocent in the name of religion. In the Nazi 'temple' upstairs, madness had masqueraded as religion and evil had been glorified.

Certain spectres are reportedly seen, while others are said to have been heard. Some can apparently make their presence felt with what seems like a physical touch, as they brush past the witnesses in an allegedly haunted corridor. Whatever haunts Wewelsburg does not fall into any of those categories. It is like a strange mixture of potent, psychic toxins that create an atmosphere rather than discernible apparitions, but it is so powerful that you do not have to be a medium to feel it.

Lionel Fanthorpe is a world renowned investigator of the psychic world, he is President of ASSAP – The Association for the Scientific Study of Anomalous Phenomena, and BUFORA – The British UFO Research Association.

For more information on Lionel and his ghostly endeavours visit his official website at www.lionel-fanthorpe.com

Above: Those who took their last ride in Allan's hearse 'Elvira' have left their impression in more ways than one...

THE HEARSE WHISPERER'S TALE

LOCATION: Sydney, Australia

DATE: January 2005

TESTIMONY: Allan The Hearse Whisperer, Destiny Tours

In late 2004 an intriguing lot appeared on eBay in Australia, inviting people to bid for a ticket to spend a night locked inside a haunted hearse. I placed the listing, which read as follows: 'Want a terrifying ghostly experience? Then bid now to win a ticket to spend a night in the world's most haunted hearse. I am auctioning a ticket for the spookiest experience of a lifetime.' Medium June Cleeland, a well-known Australian medium, said 'as a clairvoyant medium with over twenty years' professional experience, there is no doubt in my mind that Elvira is haunted. I dare anyone to spend the night inside her without experiencing some incredible phenomena.'

On offer was the chance to experience a night of dread inside 'Elvira', which is a 1967 Cadillac hearse and a veteran of over 10,000 funerals during her 30-year career with a funeral home in California. It was imported to an Australian dealer in 1997, with whom it remained until I purchased 'her' in 1999. My plan was to have her converted with seating as the transport for my Weird Sydney Ghost & History Tours. It seems, however, that during the restoration she was reborn in more ways than one.

Not long after Elvira commenced her tours, visitors who had sat in the back seats told me that they had experienced peculiar pains in the lower abdomen and a sensation of stabbing in the leg. At first this was explained as coincidence but over the years I have become convinced that she is truly haunted. On one occasion after drifting off to sleep inside her I was awoken by something stroking my face. Even car mechanics working on her have been affected by the eerie aura that surrounds the vehicle, and some of my drivers have been touched on the hand by the spirit of the old hearse driver. Apparently, he is confused by the fact that I have had the car altered to become a right-hand drive.

Numerous psychics, mediums and clairvoyants have confirmed that there are several spirits connected to the means of transport to their final resting place. Psychic Debbie Malone said: 'I can confirm that your beautiful hearse – Elvira – is definitely haunted.' Elvira has carried over 6,000 live passengers to date and hundreds of them have encountered the spirits of the vehicle's morbid past while enjoying the ride. Most of the experiences have been gentle and friendly but occasionally a smell of rotting flesh pervades the interior and an icy cold breeze drifts about.

The winning bidder for the ticket was ghost hunter Judy Krem of Southern Highlands Ghost Hunts and Investigations. She slept in the back of Elvira on a warm night, Wednesday, 12 January 2005. There was no

need for Elvira to be parked near a cemetery or any other such location, she was parked in the driveway of her owner's residence in suburban Wahroonga, Sydney.

At first Judy was accompanied by Kelly Giblin of Paranormal Australia. They noticed strange readings on their electromagnetic field meters and digital thermometers from the start. However, it was while Judy was on her own that strange things really started to occur. She described that she had heard the voices of two people coming from the driver and front passenger's seats. As this happened she switched on her digital thermometer and noted a temperature drop of -17° C. Next a distinct laugh was heard as if in reaction to the temperature reading. No one was in the vicinity. Later in the evening she watched in amazement as a ghostly blue glow immersed her feet in the foot well and a green globe of light danced along one of the windows.

After the night was over and Judy had recovered from her experiences she sent me an email thanking me for the experience. From which I quote verbatim: 'Elvira is definitely haunted, and beautiful... make sure you tell her I said that Allan... very beautiful as well!'

If you fancy taking a spin in one of Allan's haunted hearses, take a look at his website to find out how – www.destinytours.com.au

Above left: 'Elvira' (on the left) the world's most haunted hearse, and her sister 'Morticia', a 1962 Cadillac hearse/ambulance combination, also haunted by the spirits of those who died in her on the way to hospital.

Below: Ghost Hunter Judy Krem spent a night inside the haunted hearse after bidding for the experience on an internet auction site.

Above: 'Robert' the haunted doll watches all those that visit the Fort East Martello Museum in Florida, USA.

THE CASE OF THE HAUNTED DOLL

LOCATION: Fort East Martello Museum, Florida, USA

DATE: November 2004

TESTIMONY: Shaun Jones, South Florida Ghost Team

In November 2004, South Florida Ghost Team conducted an investigation at the Fort East Martello Museum located in Key West, Florida. The museum is an unfinished fort, built during the Civil War. Its walls are made of granite and are eight feet thick in some places. If you climb to the top of the tower that sits in the middle of the fort, you can enjoy a breathtaking view of the nearby coastline.

We arrived the day before the investigation and spent our time touring Key West and its environs. We visited the oldest cemetery where it is said that a vampire's grave is located, which sadly we were not able to locate. We hoped our ghost investigation at the museum would be more fruitful. There were times that yellow fever, typhoid, cholera and malaria spread through this area like wildfire, and many of those buried here had died from these diseases. A chilling legend dictates that the bodies of those interred in the graveyard will wash out of their graves during a storm, luckily for us the weather was calm.

We arrived at the Fort East Martello Museum around 9pm and placed our infrared cameras around the inside of the museum. We then met Robert, a unique three foot tall doll, who is highly regarded at the museum and has an interesting story.

In the year 1903, the doll was given to Robert Eugene Otto, or Gene as he was known, when he was four years old and he named it after himself. Gene received the doll from a Haitian girl who is said to have created the doll in Gene's likeness and placed upon it a voodoo spell. When Gene grew up he became a successful artist and the doll remained in his possession. Whenever some misfortune came his way he would blame it on 'Robert'.

When Gene got married his wife encountered strange phenomena which she believed was caused by the presence of the doll. On one occasion she was locked in the attic and on others she was attacked. One account from a visiting plumber tells how the doll hit the tradesman from behind, before sitting back in a chair. Other people reported seeing the doll wave at them from upstairs windows. With so many strange tales surrounding this old doll, we wondered if anything odd would occur in its vicinity during our investigation. As we explored, Robert watched on from his glass display case, clutching his favourite stuffed toy.

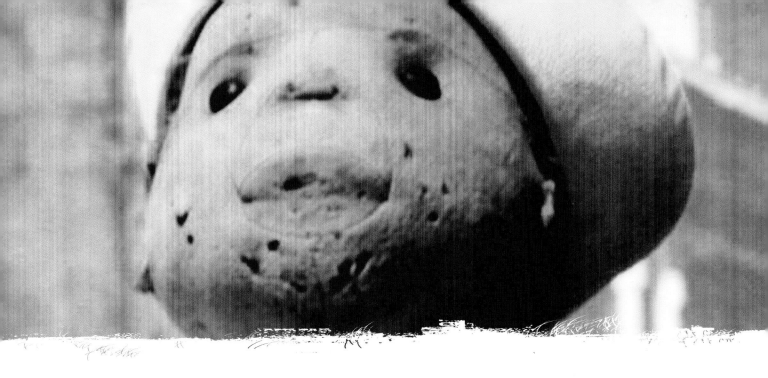

Once we had all our equipment positioned, we began to take temperature readings, electromagnetic field readings and conduct a complete tour of the museum. Later in the investigation, while viewing the monitors we noticed that one of the video cameras was moving up and down. The only way that this could occur is if someone, or something, was moving the camera physically. This incident was repeated periodically throughout the night. On one occasion I decided to walk down to the camera to see what was happening and took another investigator with me.

Below: The doll, now residing within a glass case in the Fort East Martello Museum, was given to Robert Otto when he was four years old. It had been cursed by a voodoo spell.

Above: Supernatural effects which have been witnessed inside the museum are blamed on 'Robert'.

As you might have guessed, when we reached the camera in question it was static, nor was there any sign of anything that could have moved it, so we turned around to make our way back to the monitors. As we walked back to the base area there was a sharp and pronounced tug on my right trouser leg, just above my knee. It startled me and I jumped, almost knocking my colleague over. He asked what had happened and I explained what I had felt on my leg. It was then that I realized that the doll would have been just the right height for the tug I had experienced. Was Robert causing mischief in the museum? Later in the evening another investigator encountered the same phenomena – a tug on their trouser leg from an unseen presence. We also experienced an incessant tapping and knocking from a variety of locations during the vigil. Once there was a tremendous bang on the front door and when it was opened no one was there.

After taking a break for a few minutes and sitting in the courtyard I returned to my colleagues who were busy observing the monitors, as I walked up to the door I heard a loud click. I froze on the spot and watched as the door slowly opened in front of me. At first I thought it might have been one of the team members, but as the door opened it was clear that there was no one on the other side. I walked through the doorway and asked if the investigators had seen it open – they had. They told me that they had watched as the latch was pushed down of its own volition before the door swung slowly open. By now our nerves were shattered. There was no explanation and we believed that the haunted doll was something to do with what was happening inside the building.

The rest of the night passed quietly, at one point a pocket of ice-cold air wafted around our heads before dissipating, but there were no more high jinks from Robert. At sunrise we packed up the equipment and left the museum.

Whether the legend of the doll is real or not is a matter of belief, but something of his height definitely touched us that night and something was messing around with our cameras. Could this have been Robert? Evidently, he does not like being photographed as the museum has an array of letters from museum visitors who have encountered bad luck after training their camera lenses on him. There is definitely a strange, eerie aura surrounding the doll, and we will be back again to investigate further that is, if Robert agrees.

For further details about the activities of The South Florida Ghost Team visit their website at http://floridaghostteam.com

If you fancy visiting Robert at the Fort East Martello Museum, information on their opening times can be found at www.kwahs.com/martello.htm

Below: Visitors should be wary of taking pictures of the doll; as this testimony reveals...

WARNING
Don't photograph

Robert,
I should've listened to those who warned me about photographing you. I paid for the few of the photos I took. Listed below is the trouble YOU caused me.

1. My 2 favorite souvenirs from Key West came up missing

2. Upon returning my car rental, an unexplained $50.00 charge showed up on my credit card

3. The hotel I had a reservation at, YOU gave my room to someone else

4. On my return flight home, YOU gave me the same the seat number as another passenger

5. When I went to retrieve my luggage at the airport, it wasn't on the carousel it was assigned to, YOU put it 2 carousels further down. Mine was the only one that was on the wrong carousel

6. YOU had my loving cat greet my return home by biting me

7. YOU made me late to work, on my first day back from vacation

Happy Halloween Robert

Robert the Doll

For over 100 years, Robert has been blamed for every type of misconduct.

There are many theories about why Robert behaves the way he does. Some say it is voodoo. Some say that it is an ancient curse. Still others insist that Gene Otto's ghost has returned to the doll he loved so much. Or that it has something to do with the fact that the house at 534 Eaton Street was already haunted before Gene and Robert shared it until Gene's death in 1974.

In 1903, Robert was given to the four-year-old Gene Otto. As Gene grew up he blamed everything bad on Robert; every type of misdeed, treachery and mischief.

By the time Gene was married and a successful artist, Robert had taken the blame for a lifetime of error, sin and folly. By then Robert's face had changed and his eyes became more changeable and expressive. For years Robert has been seen and heard moving around: shifting positions and giggling behind people's backs. Although well worn, Robert has not mellowed with age. Even the Fort cats keep their distance while staring at him.

It used to be that people just talked about Robert's shenanigans. But these days they have been sending more and more cards and letters. Some to apologize and some demand apologies. Robert seldom replies, but he does like keeping his fan mail.

If you want to hear the latest stories, just ask the people who work here, or if you should notice lots of things going wrong, blame it on Robert.

THE HAUNTED MANSION

LOCATION: Felt Mansion, Michigan, USA

DATE: November 2001

TESTIMONY: Nicole Bray, West Michigan Ghost Hunters Society

Felt Mansion was built by the millionaire and inventor, Dorr Eugene Felt (1862–1930). It was to be a summer home and a special gift to his wife, Agnes. Sadly, just a few short weeks after the completion of the Mansion in 1928, Agnes passed away in her room. Later Dorr remarried, but his new wife hated the house he had built for his former love, and as such the family spent most of their time in Chicago, until his death in 1930.

Following the death of Mr Felt, the mansion estate was handed over to his daughters, but they were unable to run it efficiently and so it was sold to a seminary run by nuns, and it became a school for boys. Following its success, the seminary built a three-storey boarding house on the property to house more students. In the 1960s, however, enrolment declined and the seminary was sold to the state of Michigan. The state decided that the boarding house would make an excellent correctional facility and they commissioned its alteration, creating Dunes Correctional Facility. The mansion building was used as prison offices and another outbuilding was transformed into a holding unit, which was a kind of luxury prison for the more well-behaved inmates. During the 1980s, budget cuts forced the closure of the facility and the entire site was turned over to the township for one dollar. A stipulation in the transfer dictated that the building must remain for public use and could not be sold to a private individual. It can now be rented out for weddings, parties and corporate events, and it is believed to be haunted.

West Michigan Ghost Hunters Society heard about the Felt Mansion in November 2001 and were granted permission to conduct the first of several paranormal investigations, which were held in the same month. During the first vigil, we were excited by several photographs that appeared to show ectoplasmic mists which were not seen at the time. There were also physical phenomena in the form of lights dimming in various rooms; in particular, what had been Agnes Felt's bedroom on the second floor. We were assured by the administrator that no electrical problems had ever occurred prior to our visit, and we took this as a sign that there was definitely a considerable haunted heritage at the mansion. We decided to undertake a full research project on the building, which lasted until October 2002.

The most haunted areas of the mansion seem to be Agnes' bedroom, Dorr's Study and the ballroom. It was inside Agnes' bedroom that one of our investigators was so spooked that he ran from

the scene in fear, having witnessed the French doors open of their own accord. At the time he was using a hand-held video camera and the resulting footage is humorous to say the least. In the same room, watched from outside, witnesses have seen a glowing ball of pink light float around the room and temperature fluctuations of more than 16°C have been documented here. In the ballroom we found that there were spikes of electromagnetic energy which could not be explained. Almost as if the ghostly dancers were waltzing silently and invisibly around us. The most common occurrence is the sound of disembodied footsteps which have been heard by day workers and members of the ghost investigation team.

The administrator of the mansion told us of her own encounter with one of the haunted mansion's unseen residents. She described a vaporous figure at the top of the staircase leading to the ballroom. This sighting occurred during a fire code inspection and the accompanying fire marshall, who also witnessed the apparition, fled in fear. One of our own investigators has also seen a full apparition inside the building, it came out of the floor of the study and walked through a closed door before disappearing.

In June 2002, the West Michigan Ghost Hunters Society, along with the Felt Mansion Committee, worked with a local radio station, WSNX 104.5FM, to conduct a radio ghost hunt. The show was called 'Broadway's Fear' (Broadway being the name of the radio presenter), and a contest was held to choose five listeners who would spend the night at the mansion investigating ghosts. One of the lucky, or unlucky, listeners was tasked with spending 30 minutes in the pitch black ballroom armed with only a two-way radio, a small flashlight and an EMF detector. She reported that the EMF detector was going wild and her flashlight kept dimming inexplicably. Later she was sent to Agnes Felt's bedroom, where she saw the ghostly pink glow which has been reported by others. One of the other guest investigators was sent into a room known as the Punishment Room during the time of the seminary. Here she listened as many 'people' were heard walking past the door on the way to the ballroom.

In the summer of 2002, in conjunction with the Felt Mansion Committee, we offered Felt Mansion Ghost Tours to the public, to help raise money for the restoration of the building. There were very few visitors who left the Felt Mansion without experiencing or capturing something which they could not explain. Some reported being touched, usually in Agnes' bedroom, while others watched with fascination when they heard a noise coming from the closet, which sounded as if the hangers were violently swinging back and forth.

The majority of people did not like the feeling that they got while they were in the ballroom. At first the seminary used the ballroom as a make-shift dormitory until the newer building was complete. Several restoration workers have stated that they felt as though they were constantly being watched in the room, and some went as far as refusing to work there. One woman, during a tour in August 2002, claimed to have been pushed while she was at the bottom of the stairs. A restoration worker also claimed that her nine-year-old son was pushed to the ground by an unseen entity outside of the mansion near the grotto in the gardens. The grotto was used as an outside worship area when the seminary was in use.

The last remaining building which was part of the Dunes Correctional Facility is nicknamed the 80 Man. Here we conducted several audio experiments and were lucky enough to record heavy footsteps, keys rattling, male voices speaking in hushed tones and the sound of a heavy steel door being slammed shut. On one occasion the sound of a bed being dragged across the floor was heard although no such bed exists today. We also heard the sounds of children's voices – could these be the sound of the boys who were once schooled here?

At the end of 2002 our ghost investigations came to an end as poor maintenance of the prison building had deemed it unsafe to inhabit, but our astounding results during this research project combined with the witness reports from mansion workers, the public and even the fire marshall, mean that the Felt mansion is surely one of the most haunted locations in the West Michigan region.

The West Michigan Ghost Hunters Society have their own website at http://www.wmghs.com

For information on the Felt Mansion visit their website at
http://www.ebold.com/~mansion/FeltMansion.html

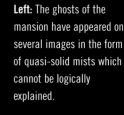

Left: The ghosts of the mansion have appeared on several images in the form of quasi-solid mists which cannot be logically explained.

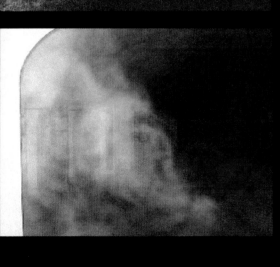

SHADOWS IN THE WINGS

LOCATION: Rogers Theatre, Wisconsin, USA

DATE: October 2003

TESTIMONY: Shawn Blaschka, Wausau Paranormal Research Society

Like many theatres, the Rogers Theatre claims to have a ghost or two. The theatre has been the site of various unexplainable phenomena and several stories have been told over the past several decades. Most of these stories are first-hand accounts that have been obtained through newspaper articles, e-mail messages to our organization and from interviews with former workers of the theatre. Apparitions, electrical disturbances, physical manifestations and the feel of veiled forces are almost commonplace here. The former theatre is well known in the area and is an important part of the community. It is situated in the historic downtown Wausau area and has had a variety of tenants over the years.

It is unclear when the original building was constructed, but historical documents indicate sometime during the second decade of the twentieth century. Records show that the building was first home to the Ammenthorp Tire Shop, with apartments located on the second floor. Although not confirmed, it is rumoured that during the early 1920s a woman was murdered in one of the apartments. In 1926 Helke's Furniture, which had been located across the street, acquired the property and it then became Helke's Funeral Home. The funeral home operated there until approximately 1939 after which the building lay vacant for a number of years. However, it was reportedly used as a brothel during this period. In 1945, it reopened as the Hollywood Theatre and then in 1960 it became the New Wausau Theatre. In 1979, it opened as the Rogers Theatre and operated as such until 2002. It came under new ownership in 2005 and at the time of writing it is being renovated as a nightclub.

Although the building officially closed its doors in 2002, many feel that the theatre is still a flurry of activity. An official paranormal investigation was conducted by the Wausau Paranormal Research Society in October 2003 and again in December 2005. The findings in 2003 were minimal but our interest at the time was increased by the fact that many witnesses had reported similar incidents in the past. Since that first investigation several more eye-witness accounts of ghost sightings have surfaced. When the Society was asked to return in December 2005, for a more extensive investigation, the findings were impressive.

The strangest events seem to occur in the basement auditorium area, where a spirit referred to by employees as Bob is said to haunt. One of the first reports was from a former staff member who was

working alone in the area. He had gone to the basement projector room to set up the film for the evening and he saw a man dressed in a black suit walk across the stage area. He checked the theatre thoroughly but no one could be found and the doors were closed and locked. Shaken by the incident, he continued his work in the projection room only to be terrified when the same man in the black suit was staring at him through the projection window. He screamed and fell to the floor in a quivering mass of panic. Minutes later he found the courage to leave the booth and fled the theatre in fear.

Another account tells of two employees that were working alone in the basement auditorium removing rows of seating. Both men heard a thumping sound from the stage area, and when they looked up they saw that the first rows of seats were bouncing. At once the men threw their tools to the floor and hurried out of the theatre, frightened by the seats rocking violently behind them as they ran. Both employees did not return that evening and refused to work alone in the building at all following the incident.

On two separate occasions the night manager was locking the front door for the evening when she was pushed from behind and fell to the ground. Several other notable phenomena have occurred during the past three decades and are as follows: lights turned on and off by unseen forces; reports of rapping noises that cannot be explained; inexplicable sounds and whispers; items being moved from one place to another; the sound of someone sitting down in the theatre seats; feelings of a strong presence; and the marquee lights turning on and off by themselves when the theatre is not occupied. Several times during matinées all five of the film projectors have turned off within seconds of each other, and when checked by an electrician no reason for the malfunction was found.

In December 2005, we returned to the theatre to perform a more thorough investigation of the site. We used several different types of instrumentation, including electromagnetic field meters, temperature probes, tape recorders for electronic voice phenomena and night-vision video recorders. During the investigation, we experienced a multitude of phenomena. Photographic anomalies were captured, including one photograph taken in one of the upstairs auditoriums which has the image of a large orb of light. The orb seems to have mass with a transparent quality.

Several researchers in our group conducted electronic voice phenomena experiments in the upstairs auditoriums during the evening with unusual results. One session recorded a female voice singing the words 'pray for you'. This voice was not heard by anyone during the recording. Just after that voice is heard on the tape, three researchers from the team witnessed a theatre chair rocking on its own. One researcher attempted to take a photograph of the chair and encountered a total loss of power to her camera. Later examination of the batteries from the camera showed that they were completely drained of power, despite being brand new at the beginning of the investigation. A second EVP session conducted in the basement and upstairs theatre areas captured more voices. The words 'Jesus Christ' were whispered very clearly on the recording.

Below: Wausau Paranormal Research Society recorded voices, apparently from ghosts, during their investigation at the Rogers Theatre.

The recordings and phenomena we experienced during the ghost investigation were objective in nature, therefore, they could not have been manufactured by those present. The building is still haunted by the shadows of those who have gone before. Let us hope the nightclub owners are not spooked easily.

For further information on Wausau Paranormal Research Society, visit their website at www.pat-wausau.org

BE AN ARMCHAIR GHOST HUNTER

If you like the idea of keeping an eye out for a ghost but don't fancy trudging around a haunted house in the dark why not take a look at these international 'GhostCams' which stream live images from the world's most haunted places straight to your personal computer via the world wide web.

At the time of writing these GhostCams were operational, but occasionally websites and web related services are suspended or cancelled. If the link no longer works try using a search engine to locate new GhostCams around the world.

ENGLAND

Ordsall Hall
http://www.salford.gov.uk/leisure/museums/ordsallhall/ghostcam.htm

Newstead Abbey
http://www.bbc.co.uk/nottingham/citylife/ghostsandlegends/spookcam.shtml

WALES

Llancaiach Fawr Manor
http://www.bbc.co.uk/wales/southeast/sites/weird/form/ghostcam.shtml

IRELAND

An Irish Linen Mill
http://www.irelandseye.com/ghost/webcam/iugeur3ig.shtm

FRANCE

The Paris Catacombs
http://www.chez.com/chriskta/webcam.htm

UNITED STATES OF AMERICA

The Willard Library
http://web.myinky.com/ghost/cam.html

The USS Lexington
http://www.caller2.com/multimedia/cams/ghostcam/main.html

The Haunted Hospital
http://www.researchwebcam.com/

The Queen Mary
http://www.ghostsandlegends.com/gl/index.php?section=ghostcam

Pennsylvania House
http://www.haunteddiary.com/genniecam.html

The Asylums Gate
http://theasylumsgate.com/Webcams.html

DIRECTORY OF GHOST HUNTERS 'THE ECTOPLASMIC YELLOW PAGES'

The following pages contain contact details for established paranormal research organisations around the world. Membership of an experienced group is a good way to begin investigating ghosts and hauntings yourself, as it has the benefit of allowing you access to the best haunted sites. Inclusion in these pages does not infer that the group has been vetted, but I have gone to some length to ensure that those included do not charge for attending their events and are not commercial enterprises.

Well-known and respected ghost hunters and groups are listed in upper case in the text – these researchers and organisations have been established for over 10 years and therefore have a good track record in the serious objective study of the paranormal.

There are other groups available, but the ones listed below are, in my opinion, the best available at the time of writing.

ENGLAND

Abbey Ghost Hunters
www.abbeyghosthunters.co.uk

Anglia Paranormal Investigation Society
www.apisteamspirit.co.uk

ASSOCIATION FOR THE SCIENTIFIC STUDY OF ANOMALOUS PHENOMENA (ASSAP)
www.assap.org

Black County Paranormal Society
www.bcps.me.uk

Bristol Society for Paranormal Research & Investigation
www.bspri.org.uk

Cambridge Ghost Investigations
www.camgi.co.uk

Cheshire Paranormal
www.cheshireparanormal.co.uk

Chesterfield Psychic Study Group
www.cpsg.co.uk

Chilterns Paranormal Research Group
www.spooks.org.uk

Club Zero
www.clubzero.co.uk

COTC Paranormal Investigations
www.cotcpi.co.uk

Derwent Paranormal Investigators
www.derwentparanormal.co.uk

E A Supernatural
www.easupernatural.com

East Anglian Paranormal
www.geocities.com/east_anglian_paranor
mal/

East Staffordshire Supernatural
Investigators
www.paranormalinvestigators.co.uk

East Sussex Paranormal Investigators
www.espi.org.uk

GHOST CLUB
www.ghostclub.org.uk

GHOST CLUB SOCIETY
www.theghostclubsociety.co.uk

Ghost Hunters UK
www.spookhunters.co.uk

Ghost Island
www.ghostisland.com
Prolific researcher: GAY BALDWIN

Ghost Research Foundation
www.jasondexterkarl.com
Prolific researcher: JASON KARL

Gloucestershire Paranormal Research
Group
www.gprg.co.uk

Harry Price Paranormal Research Group
www.harryprice.co.uk

Institute of Paranormal Research
www.iopr.org.uk

Isle of Wight Ghost Hunters
www.theisleofwightghosthunters.co.uk

Isle of Wight Ghost Investigations
www.iwgi.co.uk

Merseyside Anomalies Research
Association
www.mara.org.uk

The Myers Paranormal Society
www.parasoc.org

North Bucks Paranormal
www.northbucksparanormal.co.uk

North East Paranormal Investigation Team
http://www.npi.ontheweb.nu/

North Essex Ghost Hunters
www.northessexghosthunters.co.uk

North Surrey Paranormal Group
www.nspg.co.uk

Paranormal Investigation Team
www.pituk.co.uk

Paranormal Site Investigators
www.p-s-i.org.uk

Phoenix Paranormal Investigations
www.ppi.org.uk

Shanry Paranormal Group
www.shanry.com

SOCIETY FOR PSYCHICAL RESEARCH
www.spr.ac.uk

Spirit Seekers 2004 Paranormal
Investigation
www.spiritseekers2004.co.uk

Suffolk & Norfolk Paranormal
Investigations
http://www.geocities.com/spookhunter9/

Sussex Paranormal Investigations
www.sussexparanormalinvestigations.co.uk

Swindon Paranormal Investigation
www.ecokin.co.uk/spi

Thurrock Paranormal
www.thurrockparanormal.co.uk

UK Ghost Hunters
www.ukghosthunters.com

UK Paranormal
www.ukparanormal.co.uk

UK Paranormal Study
www.ukparanormalstudy.co.uk

Underwood, Peter
www.peterunderwood.org.uk
Prolific researcher: PETER UNDERWOOD

White Rose Paranormal
www.whiteroseparanormal.com

Worcester Paranormal Group
www.worcesterparanormalgroup.com

SCOTLAND

Alba Paranormal Investigations
www.albaparanormal.com

Ghost Finders Scotland
www.ghostfinders.co.uk

Scottish Society for Psychical Research
www.sspr.co.uk

WALES

Celtic Paranormal Investigations
www.cpi.moonfruit.com

IRELAND

Northern Ireland Psychical Society
http://www.sprni.ic24.net/site/

MALAYSIA

Malaysia Ghost Research Society
http://penyelidikanhantu.blogspot.com/

AUSTRALIA

Brisbane Ghost Hunters
members.tripod.com/~cluricaun/main.htm

Paraquest Australia Paranormal
Investigations
www.paraquestaustralia.com

Advanced Ghost Hunters of Seattle Tacoma
www.aghost.us

Alabama Foundation for Paranormal Research
www.alabamaparanormal.org

American Association of Paranormal Investigators
www.ghostpi.com

American Ghost Society
www.prairieghosts.com
Prolific researcher: TROY TAYLOR

American Society for Psychical Research
www.aspr.com

Appalachian Ghost Hunters Society
www.appalachian-ghost-hunters-society.com

Arizona Desert Ghost Hunters
www.adghosthunters.com

Aware Foundation Paranormal Research
www.angelfire.com/scifi/deliverances/index.html

Bay Area Paranormal Investigations
www.bayareaparanormal.com

California Ghost Hunters Society
www.californiaghosthunters.com

California Paranormal Society
www.californiaparanormalsociety.com

Cape & Islands Paranormal Research Society
www.caiprs.com

Central Arkansas Society for Paranormal Research
www.casprquest.com

Central Ohio Paranormal Society
www.centralohioparanormal.com

Certified Hunters In Paranormal Studies
www.chipsparanormal.com

Chester County Paranormal Research Society
www.chestercountyprs.com

Connecticut Paranormal Research Society
http://www.cprs.info/

Crawford County Ghost Hunters
www.crawfordcountyghosthunters.com

Dagulf's Ghost Paranormal
www.dagulfsghost.com

DFW Paranormal Research of North Texas
www.dfwparanormalresearch.com

East Coast Paranormal Investigation Team
www.ecpitghosthunters.com

Eastern Paranormal
www.easternparanormal.com

Florida Paranormal Research Foundation
www.floridaparanormal.com

Ghost Hunters of South Michigan
www.ghosm.com

Ghost Investigators Society
www.ghostpix.net

Ghost Research Society
www.ghostresearch.org
Prolific researcher: DALE KACZMAREK

Ghost Seekers of Central New York
www.cnyghost.com

Ghost Seekers of Michigan
www.ghostseekers-of-michigan.com

Ghoststudy
www.ghoststudy.com

Idaho Spirit Seekers
www.idahospiritseekers.com

Indiana Paranormal Investigations
www.indianaparanormal.com

Infinity Paranormal
www.infinityparanormal.com

International Ghost Hunters Society
www.ghostweb.com
Prolific researchers: DAVE OESTER & SHARON GILL

INTERNATIONAL SOCIETY FOR PARANORMAL RESEARCH (ISPR)
www.ispr.net

Isis Paranormal Investigations
www.isisinvestigations.com

Louisville Ghost Hunters Society
www.louisvilleghs.com

Maine's Paranormal Research Association
www.mainesparanormal.com

Memphis Ghost Hunters
www.memphisghosthunters.com

Metroplex Paranormal Investigations
www.metroplexparanormalinvestigations.com

Miller Paranormal Research
www.millersparanormalresearch.com

Missouri Ghost Hunters Society
www.ghosthaunting.com

Missouri Paranormal Research Society
www.missouriparanormal.com

Moonlight Ghost Hunters
www.moonlightghosthunters.com

New England Paranormal
www.newenglandparanormal.com

New England Society for Psychic Research
www.warrens.net
Prolific researchers: ED & LORRAINE WARREN

New Hampshire Paranormal Research Group
www.angelfire.com/ne2/nhprg/index4.htm

New Jersey Ghost Research
www.njgr.org

North Florida Paranormal Research Inc.
www.ghosttracker.com

Northwest Ghost Hunters
www.nwgh.com

Northwest Ohio Paranormal Research Group
www.noprg.com

Ohio EVP & Paranormal Society
www.ohioevp.com

Oklahoma City Ghost Club
www.okcgc.com

ParaHaunt
www.miparahaunt.com

Paranormal Researchers of Ohio Valley
www.proov.net

Paranormal Research Society of New
England
www.prsne.com

Paranormal Research Society of Texas
www.paranormal.texas.net

Para Researchers of Ontario
www.pararesearchers.org

Philadelphia Ghost Hunters Alliance
www.phillyghost.com

Proof Paranormal
www.proofparanormal.com

PSI Paranormal Scientific Investigations
www.psiparanormal.com

Psychokinetic Energy Investigations
www.geocities.com/bmore_ghosts/

San Diego Ghost Hunters
www.sandiegoghosthunters.com

San Gabriel Valley Paranormal
Researchers
www.sgvpr.org

Scientific Investigative Ghost Hunting
Team
www.sightonline.com

Sigil Paranormal
www.sigilparanormal.com

Society for paranormal Interests &
Research Investigation Team
www.spirit-search.com

Soul Trackers
www.soultrackers.com

Southern California Ghost
Hunters Society
www.scghs.com

South Florida Ghost Team
www.floridaghostteam.com

South Jersey Ghost Research
www.sjgr.org

Spirit Investigations
www.spiritinvestigations.net

Spirit Quest Paranormal
www.spiritquestparanormal.com

THE ATLANTIC PARANORMAL SOCIETY
(TAPS)
www.the-atlantic-paranormal-society.com

The Centre for Paranormal Research
www.virginiaghosts.com

The Paranormal Society of Pennsylvania
www.paranormalpa.com

The Shadowlands Ghost Hunters
www.scghosthunters.com

Toronto Ghosts 7 Hauntings
Research Society
www.torontoghosts.org

Triangle Paranormal Investigations
www.triangleparanormal.com

Washington DC Metro Area
Ghost Watchers
www.dchauntings.com

Wausau Paranormal Research Society
www.pat-wausau.org

West Virginia Ghost Hunters
www.westvirginiaghosthunters.com

BIBLIOGRAPHY

Jason Karl's Great Ghost Hunt
Jason Karl

The Illustrated History of the Haunted World
Jason Karl

Prestbury Haunts
Jason Karl

The Haunted Places of Lancashire
Jason Karl

On the Trail of The Ghosts of Pluckley
Sarah Ann Kerr

Haunted Pluckley
Dennis Chambers

The Ghosts of Pluckley
Anthony Sedlacek & Chris Slade

Ghosts & How To See Them
Peter Underwood

Haunt Hunters Guide to Florida
Joyce Elson Moore

ACKNOWLEDGEMENTS

I must firstly thank my Publishing Manager Jo Hemmings for believing in this project and for her support over the past year, and my editor at New Holland, Charlotte Judet. My thanks must also go to Derek Acorah for his wonderful foreword and to Gwen, his lovely wife. I am also indebted to Sian Rayner, the researcher on this project.

In particular I must thank in each case:

The Castle of Whispers – Testimony written by Stuart Andrews of the Paranormal Research Organisation. Photography by Stuart Andrews.

At Her Majesty's Pleasure – Testimony written by Dave Wood and Nicky Sewell of Paranormal Site Investigators. Photography by Paranormal Site Investigators.

The Haunted Holiday Cottage – Testimony of Suzanne Williams written by Jason Karl. Photography by the Ghost Research Foundation.

Caught on Film – Testimony of Martin Finch written by Jason Karl, with thanks to Sally and Bruce Thomson. Photography by John Mason and the Ghost Research Foundation. Ghost photograph supplied by kind permission of Martin Finch.

Yo-Ho, Yo-Ho, A Haunting Life for Me! – Testimony written by Stuart Andrews of Haunting Experiences. Photography by Stuart Andrews.

All Manor of Secrets... – Testimony of Veronica Charles written by Jason Karl. Photography by the Ghost Research Foundation.

Ghost Island – Testimony written by Gay Baldwin. Photography by Gay Baldwin.

Patients From the Past – Testimony written by Paul Gerfen of Myths, Ghosts & Legends. Photography by Paul Gerfen.

The Antiquarian Apparition – Testimony of Jim Rice and Len Webb written by Jason Karl, with thanks to Bourne Mill. Photography by the Ghost Research Foundation, ghost photograph supplied by kind permission of Jim Rice and Len Webb.

Most Haunted? – Testimony written by Paul Howse of the Ghost Research Foundation, with thanks to Dennis Chambers and all members of the Ghost Research Foundation who took part. Photography by the Ghost Research Foundation and Colin Smith, Andrew Ball and Denise Smith of Spiritquest.

The Spectre in the Chapel – Testimony written by Chris Howley of the Gloucestershire Paranormal Research Group. Photographs supplied by kind permission of the Woodchester Mansion Trust, ghost photograph supplied by kind permission of Andy Mercer of the Institute of Paranormal Research.

In Harry Price's Footsteps – Testimony written by Dean White. Ghost photography supplied by kind permission of Dean White.

Ghost in the Machine – Testimony of Joanne Gailey written by Jason Karl. Photography by Joanne Gailey, ghost printout supplied by kind permission of Joanne Gailey.

The Phantom Hitchhiker – Testimony written by Andrew Homer. Photography by Andrew Homer and Dr David Simones-Jones.

House of Hell – Testimony of Angela Borrows written by Jason Karl. Photography by the Ghost Research Foundation. Ghost photographs supplied by kind permission of John Riley.

Lily's Story – Testimony written by Adele Yeomans. Photography by the Ghost Research Foundation and Abigail & Eye Photographers.

The Psychic Museum – Testimony written by Lionel Fanthorpe. Photography by The Psychic Museum.

Horror Hotel – Testimony of Phylip De La Maziere written by Jason Karl. Photography by the Ghost Research Foundation.

The Children of the Mine – Testimony written by Mark & Angela Riley of Abbey Ghost Hunters. Photography by Abbey Ghost Hunters.

The Spectre Inspectors – Testimony written by Rachel Bell of Ghost N Spectres. Photography by Paul McDonald.

Touched By The Dead – Testimony written by Nicole Sheldon of UK Haunted. Photography by the Ghost Research Foundation.

Walled Up Alive – Testimony of Veronica Charles written by Jason Karl. Photography by the Ghost Research Foundation.

Ghosts of the Forgotten Lane – Testimony written by Ryan O'Neill of Scottish Paranormal. Photographs supplied by kind permission of Karen Baron Heritage Projects, photographs by Gary Doak.

A Face in the Window – Testimony written by Stephen Lambert of Charity Ghost Hunts. Photography by Andrew Johnson. Ghost photograph supplied by kind permission of Stephen Lambert.

Terror Tower – Testimony written by Ryan O'Neill of Scottish Paranormal. Photography by Scottish Paranormal.

Hidden Haunts – Testimony written by Jason Karl. Photography by the Ghost Research Foundation.

The Haunted Gite – Testimony of Jane Powers, written by Jason Karl. Photography by the Ghost Research Foundation.

The Monk of Carcassonne – Testimony of Phylip De La Maziere written by Jason Karl. Photographs supplied by kind permission of The Carcassonne Corporation.

Tormented Souls – Testimony written by Lionel Fanthorpe. Photography by Lionel Fanthorpe.

The Hearse Whisperer's Tale – Testimony written by Allan the Hearse Whisperer. Photography by Destiny Tours.

The Case of the Haunted Doll – Testimony written by Shaun Jones of the South Florida Ghost Team. Photography by Shaun Jones.

The Haunted Mansion – Testimony written by Nicole Bray of West Michigan Ghost Hunters Society. Photography by West Michigan Ghost Hunters Society.

Shadows in the Wings – Testimony written by Shawn Blaschka of Wausau Paranormal Research Society. Photography by Shawn Blaschka.

A

Abbey Ghost Hunters 100–3
Acorah, Derek 8
Addicoat, Ian 29
Age of Aquarius 11
Allan the Hearse Whisperer 138–9
Alvanos, Nick 59, 63
Andrews, Stuart
    Pengersick Castle, Cornwall 14–17
    Smuggler's Haunt Hotel, Devon 28–31
Association for the Scientific Study of Anomalous Phenomena 92
Association for the Scientific Study of Phenomena Parasearch 80–1
Atkins, Gloria 67

B

Babbs, Edward 75, 76
Baillie of Letham, General William 122–3
Baldwin, Gay 38–43
Bandon, Billy 68
Battle of Sourton (1643) 25
Bell, Rachel 104–7
Bere, Jim and Daphne 67, 68
Bibliography 156
Black Horse Inn, Pluckley 51, 52, 54, 57–63
Blacksmiths Arms, Pluckley 59, 67–8
Blaschka, Shawn 148–51
Bodmin Gaol, Cornwall 18–21
Bolton, John and Ellen 82
Borley Rectory, Suffolk 74–7
Borley Rectory - The Final Analysis (Babbs) 75
Borrows, Angela 82–5
Botanical Gardens, Ventnor, Isle of Wight 44–7
Bourne Mill, Surrey 48–9
Bray, Nicole 144–7
Brickworks, Pluckley 65

Bridgnorth, Shropshire 80–1
Brooke, Rupert 8
Brown, Paul 51, 61
Bucknall, Benjamin 70
Bull, Reverend Henry Dawson Ellis 74
Bury, Charles William 128
Buss, John 52
Buss, Richard 62, 66

C

Cainerer, Jonathan 92
Campbell, Cheryl 114
Carcassonne, France 132–5
Castle Cary, Falkirk 122–3
Castle Keep, Newcastle Upon Tyne 104–7
Chambers, Dennis 51, 55–6, 59–60, 62
Charities Trust 82
Charity Ghost Hunts 122–3
Charles, Veronica
    Monkton Old Hall, Pembrokeshire 114–17
    Pluckley, Kent 51, 54–6, 57, 59, 65, 67–8
    Stanford Orcas Manor, Dorset 32–7
Charleville Forest Castle, County Offaly 126–9
Claridge, Colonel 32
Cleeland, June 138
Cleveland Ironstone Mining Museum, Teeside 100–3
Clock Tower, Fife 124–5
Cobb, J. R. 114
Cockersand Abbey 87
Craig, Wendy 51, 52
Creasey, Frank 39–43

D

Dalston, John 108
Dalston Hall Hotel, Cumbria 108–13
De La Maziere, Phylip
    The Golden Fleece Inn, York 96–9

Monk of Carcassonne 132–5
Dering Arms, Pluckley 51, 59, 3–4, 68
Destiny Tours 138–9

Dicky Buss's Lane, Pluckley 62–3
Dunes Correctional Facility 144, 146

E

Elliott, Bob 29
Elvey Farm, Pluckley 66

F

Fanthorpe, Lionel
    The Psychic Museum, York 92–5
    Wewelsburg Castle, Germany 136–7
Felt, Agnes 144–5
Felt, Dorr Eugene 144
Felt Mansion, USA 144–7
Finch, Martin 24–7
Fletcher, Les 39, 43
Fort East Martello Museum, USA 140–3
Fright Corner, Pluckley 66

G

Gailey, Joanne 78
Gambling, Laura 57
Garley, Andrew 51, 52, 54, 56, 57, 59–60, 62
Garlick, Stuart 80–1
Geller, Uri 92
Gerfen, Paul 44–7
Ghost Club of London 74
Ghost Hunters 152–5
Ghost-N-Spectres 104–7
Ghost Research Foundation 126
    Highwayman Inn, Devon 25–6
    Pluckley, Kent 50–69

GhostCams 152
Giblin, Kelly 139
Gloucestershire Paranormal
    Research Group 70–3
Godyton, Walter de 38
Golden Fleece Inn, York 96–9
Grenfell, R. T. 39
Grenham, Sir Thomas 108
Greystones, Pluckley 64

H

Hansom, Charles 70
Haunting Experiences 14–17
Hearse Whisperer, The 138–9
Heavey-Seaquist, Constance
    126
Hesketh, William 87
Highwayman Inn, Devon 24–7
Hitchhiker, Phantom 80–1
Hobs Reprographics, Coventry
    78
Holmes, Daniel 69
Homer, Andrew 80–1
Hough, Kevin 51
Howley, Chris 70–3
Howse, Paul 50–69
Hugh-Adelaide, Harriet 128
Hynes, Kevin 29–30

I

Institute of Paranormal
    Research 72

J

Jarvis, Diana 51, 52, 57, 67
Johnston, Francis 126
Jones, Buster 24
Jones, Shaun 140–3
Jones, W. E. 39

K

Karl, Jason
    Charleville Forest
        Castle, County Offaly
        126–9

Pluckley, Kent 51, 62, 69
Keast-Marriott, Andy 51, 57,
    60, 62
Kingston-Miles, Ted 59
Krem, Judy 138–9

L

Lambden Cottage, Pluckley
    68
Lambert, Stephen 122–3
Lampert, Bridget 51, 52
Lampert, James 51
Landmark Trust
    Margells, Devon 22–3
    Monkton Old Hall,
        Pembrokeshire 114
Leigh, William 70
Leonard, Tom 100
Ley lines
    Charleville Forest Castle,
        County Offaly 126
    Pengersick Castle, Cornwall
        15
    Pluckley, Kent 52, 67
Lighthouse Dwelling, Isle of
    Wight 40–3
Lodge St Jeanne d'Arc,
    Carcassonne 133–4
Low, Lenny 124, 125
Lumley, Joanna 11

M

Madeley, Richard 11
Mains Hall, Lancashire 86–91
Malone, Debbie 138
Margells, Devon 22–3
Mary King's Close, Edinburgh
    118–21
Mason, John 51
Maynard, Anthony Lax 100
McMullen, Michael 126
Meddlycott, Sir Mervyn 34, 36
Mercer, Andrew 72
Meschines, Robert de 108
Miles, Norie 51, 61, 62
Milner, Wendy 71
Monk of Carcassonne 132–5

Monkton Old Hall,
    Pembrokeshire 114–17
Myths, Ghosts & Legends
    44–7

N

National Trust 70
Noyle, Edward 33

O

Obraszowa, Maja 12
Okey, Samuel Frederick 100
Old Bakery, Pluckley 64
O'Neill, Ryan
    Clock Tower, Fife 124–5
    Mary King's Close,
        Edinburgh 118–21
O'Regan, Elaine 51
Otto, Robert Eugene 140–3

P

Paranormal Australia 139
Paranormal Research
    Organisation 14
Paranormal Site Investigators
    18–21
Park Wood, Pluckley 68
Peckett, Lady Alice 98
Pengersick Castle, Cornwall
    14–17
Perrott, Tom 76
Phantom Hitchhiker 80–1
Piscean age 11
Pittock, Reverend John 56
Pluckley, Kent 50–69
Powers, Jane 130–1
Price, Harry 74
Psychic Museum, York 92–5
Psychic News 11
Pugin, Augustus 70

R

Raby's Farm, Lancashire 82–5
Rayner, Sian 51
Reagan, Ronald 12

Resurrection Bob 29
Rice, Jim 48–9
Riley, Angela 100–3
Riley, John 83–4
Riley, Mark 100–3
Robinson, Tom 100
Rogers Theatre, USA 148–51
Rose Court, Pluckley 64
Royal National Hospital for
    the Diseases of the Chest,
    Ventnor 44–7
Russell, Natalie 62–3

S

Sandford Orcas Manor, Dorset
    32–7
Scottish Paranormal
    Clock Tower, Fife 124–5
    Mary King's Close,
        Edinburgh 118–21
Screaming Man, the 65
Screaming Woods, Pluckley 66
Sewell, Nicky 18–21
Shaw, Thomas 82
Sheldon, Nicole 108–13
Simms, Anthony 15
Smuggler's Haunt Hotel,
    Devon 28–31
South Florida Ghost Team
    140–3

Southern Highland Ghost
    Hunts and Investigations
    138–9
Speakman, Reverend Wilfred
    82
St Alban's Abbey 114
St Catherine's Lighthouse, Isle
    of Wight 38–43
St Nicholas' Churchyard,
    Pluckley 52–6
Stewart, Sheila 128
Swayle, Tristan 71
Sydney, Australia 138–9

T

Telepneff, Lyndi 51
Thompson, Muriel 114, 116
Thomson, Sally 24
Tomkins, C. 39
Trinity House Service 38
Turff, Henry 62

U

UK Haunted 108–13
Underwood, Peter 69

V

Vallibus, Robert de 108

Vance, Bridget 126
Vendée, France 130–1
Ventnor Botanical Gardens,
    Isle of Wight 44–7

W

Watercress Lady, The 65
Wausau Paranormal Research
    Society 148–51
Webb, Len 48–9
Webcams, ghost 152
West Michigan Ghost Hunters
    Society 144–7
Wewelsburg Castle, Germany
    136–7
White, Dean 74–7
Williams, Suzanne 22–3
Windmill, Pluckley 66
Winfred, George 56
Wood, Dave 18–21
Woodchester Mansion,
    Gloucestershire 70–3

Y

Yeomans, Adele 86–91